Dear New Carer

Carer

THINGS I KNOW NOW I WISH I KNEW THEN

Ali Jeffries

First published 2021

Published by Forward Thinking Publishing

Text © Ali Jeffries 2021

The moral rights of the author have been asserted.

All rights reserved. No part of this book may be reproduced by any mechanical, photographic, or electronic process, or in the form of a phonographic recording; nor may it be stored in a retrieval system, transmitted or otherwise be copied for public or private use, other than for 'fair use' as brief quotations embodied in articles and reviews, without prior written permission of the publisher.

The information given in this book should not be treated as a substitute for professional medical advice; always consult a medical practitioner. Any use of information in this book is at the reader's discretion and risk. Neither the author nor the publisher can be held responsible for any loss, claim, or damage arising out of the use, or misuse, of the suggestions made, the failure to take medical advice, or for any material on third party websites.

A catalogue record for this book is available from the British Library.

ISBN: 978-1-8380445-3-4

To my wonderful husband and our two gorgeous boys, your belief in me, your unwavering support, and your willingness to share has made this possible. I am so very proud of all of you.

And to Jinny, my wonderful friend, and a true cheerleader. Thank you.

Contents

Foreword

Eight years ago, my husband and I were thrown into the 'eye of the storm'.

Our family had already had its share of challenges, but the situation facing us was something quite different.

Like so many parents whose children struggle with mental and physical health issues, we felt entirely unprepared by anything we had learnt or experienced before.

During this time, we were to experience a feeling of utter helplessness. The helplessness which comes from seeing someone you love so deeply struggle so hard while you stand on the side-lines without the first clue of how to help.

My husband and I did our best to care for our boys, who were 9 and 16 at the time. As we pleaded with outside agencies for proper care, life continued with its work to be done and bills to be paid.

The rollercoaster we were on seemed never-ending and relentless.

During these years I learnt many things, mainly through trial and error. I wanted to share those successes, hoping it would help other parent carers who find themselves in a similar position.

With that in mind, I decided to start a support group and I will talk about that more later.

During the time the group was running, I was privileged to meet some amazing parent carers all with their own heart-rending stories.

It was here that I learnt an important lesson.

Our journeys were similar, but as we are individuals our perspectives are quite different. Our children are also individuals and that in turn makes for different outcomes too.

I have come to understand that there is no right or wrong way of doing things.

I know as a parent I have made my fair share of errors, but as my wise Gran would say the important thing is what we can learn from our mistakes, and that as we move forward, we can make positive changes along the way.

No-one has written a Haynes manual to help when it comes to our children or young people we care for, but if we approach things from a place of love, I really believe we are doing everything we can.

As I write this our world is in the middle of the Covid-19 pandemic and as such we are having to adapt to the way we live. For many carers, that means dealing with a lot of additional pressures.

More than ever when parents are in danger of being overwhelmed whilst caring for their children with their mental and physical health issues, I felt it was important to get this all down for you.

I want more than anything to try and be a voice of calm and hope amid whatever storm you may find yourself in by sharing some ideas, tips, and tricks that may just help.

After looking back on my journey and speaking to other parents dealing with often seemingly impossible situations, the one common factor has quite simply, and a little surprisingly, been hope.

Hope for a brighter future, relationships to be healed, empathetic professionals and, much, much better days to come.

For me, these are the days when I would have the time and energy to sit down and write a book.

It is my hope that amid your own personal journeys with all the chaos, you have days when you have the time and energy to sit down and read it.

While you do that, Dear Parent Carer, please remember what a fantastic job you are doing and how utterly amazing you are!

Self-Care in the Eye of the Storm

BEFORE WE START, I just wanted to say right from the outset, parent to parent, that regardless of what you are going through with your children and their health concerns, there is hope. I am sorry that you find yourself in that position and I see you. I would really like to try and help and the best way I know how is to share a little of my journey with you.

In this first section I will introduce you to the idea of self-care, and more importantly how incredibly beneficial it can be to you and your family.

And to kick it off I will start by telling you two things.

Firstly, regardless of what is going on in your life now, you and your feelings, your worries, and your well-being matter too. And secondly, even though at times it may feel like it, you are not on your own. Not anymore.

CHAPTER 1

It's all about you too

AS BUSY PARENTS, VERY often the notion of taking time for ourselves may be something we dream of. Anything other than the basics such as hygiene, sleeping and, eating are likely to be right at the bottom of our to-do list.

As a parent caring for children with severe mental and physical health concerns, and who has struggled with my own health, I have come to realise how beneficial and pretty much essential it was, and still is, to look after myself too.

Understanding what self-care is and how to apply it can really help when you are in a stressful situation and can be a huge aid to recovery.

I have met many parents who have struggled with the notion that caring for their children is the *be-all and end-all*. Most believe that there is no time to consider their own emotions and feelings. Very often we have a sense of misplaced guilt and I have heard many parents say:

'It's not about me, it's about my kids.'

But it is about you too!

If you are not well and run into the ground, everything seems even more dark and insurmountable. Like walking uphill in treacle.

There are many things I know now that I wish I knew then, and this book is my way of sharing this knowledge with you.

The knowledge that includes outcomes of trial and error, tried and tested methods, experiences, and practical ways you can make life a little easier while you are supporting your children.

I will share with you what self-care is, what it may look like practically and, how to practise this both when you are in the eye of the storm and also on the other side as we investigate recovery and beyond.

More importantly, I would like to show you how to practise it all *guilt-free.*

During the last 8 years, I have come across simple things that have been a good aid when supporting my children. The huge bonus is that not only have they been useful in making my children's day a little more bearable, but they have really helped me too.

Being a parent is not easy and the sort of *extreme parenting* we find ourselves in when we are looking after children with health issues can sometimes feel impossible. But hang in there, you are not on your own and there is support available, from family and friends to national charities. I would like to help you tap into it all.

It is my hope that when you have read this book, you will feel more able to face the storm with your armour upgraded, and the appropriate ammunition. More importantly, your self-worth will be intact, and you will have growing confidence in what an incredible job you are doing.

So why did I write this book?

I have found talking about my experiences and sharing my journey with others has not only helped them but has been an incredible catalyst to my own healing.

There have been many times in recent years when I have said *I wish I had known that then* and it occurred to me that the little bit of wisdom I have picked up over the years may well be of help to you too.

I want to share with you how you can do little things to look after yourself when you are feeling battle weary. How to adjust to life, and the importance of being kind and gentle to that fragile person who has just emerged from the other side of the storm.

I want to show you that asking for help is healthy and there is no shame in needing support from medical professionals as well as family and friends and your wider support network.

I also understand that as a parent, having some practical ideas to help make life better for your children brings a special type of peace, and I want to share some ideas of things you might try to this end too.

How can you use this book?

I have this idea that just as we have a first aid kit for our physical needs, we could do with one for our psychological needs as well. This kit may include things that you can just lay your hands on quickly when the need arises and could be anything from useful telephone numbers to practical things to do to help you relax.

So, you could look at this book as a pick and mix. You could choose the things that may work for you and put together a kit that is tailored to you and your situation. We will look at your kit first.

Later in the book in section 2, we can have a look at the sort of things you could put in a kit for your child.

I want to reassure you that recovery is an ongoing process. Even when we feel we are taking two steps forward and three backwards, that's ok because regardless of how slow the progress may seem to you, you're still moving in the right direction.

To keep that progress going, to help you put one foot in front of the other if that is all you can manage right now, in the next chapter I will introduce you to the idea of self-care.

I would really like you to start entertaining the idea that YOU matter and show you how important it is to look after yourself as well as your child.

Right from the outset, I want you to know that the business of self-care is not just something else to add to your ever-growing to-do list, in fact, it may just help you cross some things off.

CHAPTER 2

The What and Why of Self-Care

WHAT IS THE DICTIONARY definition of self-care?

"The practise of taking an active role in protecting one's own well-being and happiness in particular during periods of stress."

I am sure you will read that, and your parent default setting will tell you that:-

I don't have time for that.

Or

I have so much on my plate already caring for my child.

Or

I am fine, and anyway it's not about me.

Yep – I thought so. Please don't beat yourself up about that because I had exactly that initial reaction.

It has also been the same with every parent I have spoken to, who has found themselves in the position of carer extraordinaire.

From my experience, understanding what my body needed and giving myself some love too was a game-changer.

When I was up to my neck in whatever life had thrown at me, I learnt that curling into a ball in a dark corner or sticking my head in the sand was just not going to cut it.

Initially, my thoughts were that if there was nothing I could do to help my child feel better, then there was nothing I can do. I was under the false impression that I had no control over anything that was happening and for that matter truly little influence.

Indeed, we often learn the hard way but the knowledge we attain during that journey is so valuable in our lives going forward. The inventor of the light bulb, Thomas Edison said:-

"I have not failed. I've just found 10,000 ways that won't work".

What a great way to look at life.

Once I had uncurled and removed myself from the dark corner and finally found the courage to remove my head from the sand, (which was one of the ways I found did not work), I realised that I did actually have some control after all.

This was *control over my own actions.* I had figured out what did not work, so perhaps doing the opposite was the way forward.

This is the point at which I started looking after myself. It is not something that came naturally but my incentive was - if I am relatively fit and well, I will be in a much better place to care for others.

I think that, perhaps, sharing a little psychology and some things I have learnt may help illustrate this for you.

Last Night NETFLIX Saved My Life

I once had a parent compare the day that they had just been through to the plot of a disaster movie. I think it explains the intensity very well.

I am sure you will also appreciate that when you are dealing with trauma, there is no sudden satisfactory heart-warming conclusion as there is in the movies.

There is no sun shining on a peaceful neighbourhood, with the reporters and emergency services milling around and a lovely calm feel of reconciliation and a new start.

In fact, for that parent, and perhaps you can identify with this as well, the fires were still raging, the volcano was still mid eruption, the earthquake damage was still snaking across the landscape swallowing everything in its path and the 'nasties' were still waiting in the dark just around the corner.

You and your child may, like me, have experienced incredibly intense and distressing moments in your journey already. I see you. I have found that one of the benefits of talking to someone like-minded is that you do not need to spell things out and they don't need all the ins and outs (because sometimes that is someone else's story). They will understand because sadly they are likely to have been through something similar.

During times like these, we all feel extraordinarily strong emotions, but there is something going on in our subconscious as well that adds fuel to the fire.

We have been built with a very efficient system that when it works well it ensures we are able to react appropriately to a threat. We have our early ancestors to thank for this. Reacting appropriately to the situation they found themselves in was essential to their very survival. When the caveman had been in an altercation with a saber-toothed tiger the adrenalin coursing through their bodies ensured they had the stamina for the duration of the battle.

It is the same for us today, when we are in the middle of trauma our adrenalin is pumping furiously around our bodies, sometimes literally enabling us to put one foot in front of the other.

It is not a surprise therefore when you look at what is going on with us internally, that going through something like caring for a very poorly child and seeing someone you love struggle can be an exhausting experience both physically and mentally.

However, there comes a point where the initial threat is gone, the adrenalin levels suddenly subside. When I experienced this, I would find myself in this strange state of exhaustion.

I remember feeling like my whole body was demanding sleep, but I was just *past it*. I was too caught up in my worries. There was too much adrenaline from the trauma of the day to settle myself, but at the same time, I was too tired to think in sentences.

It was in moments like this when the alternative would have been hours tossing and turning and looking at the clock, that I fell in love with NETFLIX and the hours of pure escapism that lay therein.

I took this time to consciously recharge and rest, even though I was not sleeping, I could just take some time for myself.

When I could not be a carer, I had to use that care for myself. Although it was a huge effort to switch off and stop worrying, I made a conscious effort to tell myself that there is nothing I can do right now for my child, but I can do something for myself.

Once I had learnt to switch off, I could lose myself in hospital dramas or be taken in by seemingly unsolvable crimes or be transported to other worlds and this became my twilight refuge.

I became uneasy friends with the dark and twisty Meredith, I adored and tolerated Gregory House in equal measures and sat around the table and hung onto every word from Reid and Rossi as they profiled the Killer.

Some misinformed professor somewhere may have said binge-watching, much like binge anything, may be damaging to our health but knowing I had only watched 20 out of the hundreds of episodes available to me and seeing all those unwatched seasons laid out before me was a strange but huge comfort.

I would have been tired the next day anyway, but for those hours I had spent living someone else's life, I had the motivation at least to face the day ahead.

I had realised that even if I were not tucked up in bed snoring, I could still rest, and it was ok that that rest looked a little different.

I had found that getting lost in a Netflix drama was a way of coping that worked for me and it was the first thing I was able to add to my first aid kit. I also realised that it was often just the remarkably simple things that made the difference. Even now if things are a little difficult for whatever reason I will re-visit one of my favourite dramas and pick an episode and just allow myself some timeout.

I am also very lucky that I find a lot of pleasure in art and I will share a bit more about what the benefits are to having a creative outlet even if you are not blessed with the talents of Van Gogh or Monet later on in the book.

I know parents who have taken up all sorts of things from crochet to journaling, from gardening to learning a new skill online as it was something they could just pick up and focus on in those moments of calm. My husband's therapy was rebuilding and repairing his Land Rover, the garage was his *fortress of solitude* and at the time it was essential for his mental health.

Even in the midst of your own *disaster* movie, it is important to find a cave to shelter in or your own Faraday cage, somewhere that for a little while you can find some solace, whatever is good for your well-being.

As you can see self-care can look different for everyone. In its simplicity, it is about finding your baseline, your normal, and knowing how to regulate when things start moving from there. I will explain a little more about how to do that in the next chapter.

CHAPTER 3

Finding Your Normal

THERE IS A SAYING that my Nanny would use quite often and that is *a stitch in time saves nine*. If you apply it to something as serious as your health you can see it makes a lot of sense.

In order to know when that *stitch* needs applying, I have found that you first have to be aware of your baseline and what is normal for you.

Unless you are an athlete or someone who constantly relies on being in *tiptop* condition it is not something we think about naturally. It is something that we have to be consciously aware of especially when as parent carers, understandably we feel our priority is to look out for our children.

Say for instance your normal is that you very rarely suffer from headaches and if you do a couple of mild painkillers ensure you can get straight back to what you were doing. But what if you have another the following day, you may well say, *well with everything I am going through its hardly surprising.* The following day the headache returns, and the mild painkillers are just not cutting it. At what point do you say, *this is not my normal, maybe I should just check it out?*

I am going to take a risk and say that if you are in the middle of trauma with your child, you are likely to ignore it until it becomes a real problem. I am not saying that we should all become hypochondriacs overnight, just that it is important to be aware and go with our gut instinct if we feel something is wrong sooner rather than later. Unfortunately, I learnt the hard way as you will see. However, I did learn and now I am healthily aware if something is a bit off. If nothing else a trip to the doctor may just allow some peace of mind and, as we have discussed, any peace is worth grabbing with both hands.

I have learnt that it is so important to know what my normal is and as you can see from the experience I am about to share with you, it is worth figuring that out early on.

The benefit of ensuring that you are in the best health possible is that you stand a better chance of coming out of the trauma you find yourself in with the least possible damage.

When I ignored the signs

During the period when we were dealing with so many challenges, my health really suffered. I was diagnosed with stress-related ME and Fibromyalgia. I established that there is no definitive test available and the only way that a diagnosis can be made is if all the other things that present with similar symptoms are ruled out. When I was told the news, it was one of those moments when someone puts into words what you have been trying to deny.

I felt a whole spectrum of emotions. I was immensely grateful that even as debilitating as the condition could be at least it was not something a lot more serious, and that's nothing compared to what I was already going through. But niggling behind this façade of *I can cope with anything, just bring it on* was the frightening reality that this intense fatigue was not just lack of sleep and something I was constantly hopeful I could remedy. I was pretty much out of emotional strength and now this new curve ball was on a course to take out my physical strength too, and at a point where I probably needed it the most.

I could just about function enough to do what I had to do now. All the accounts I had read about both the illnesses, described deterioration to a point of being bed-bound. I asked myself, *how on earth was I going to cope?*

My younger son had his own health issues and therefore needed therapy three times a week. Working with the little energy I had was a momentous task. At this time, my week looked something like this.

We would get to the hospital and try and find a parking space near the children's wing. We had managed to hire a reasonably light wheelchair but hauling this out of the boot of my car was incredibly difficult. I was out of breath and feeling sick and dizzy even before we had started.

There was also the emotional side of seeing my son in pain as the kind, but firm staff tried to help him slowly build up his strength. Once this was over, I had to push him in his wheelchair often still in tears from the exertion of the appointment up the hill as most of the car parks were built on higher ground. By the time I had done that and got him safely in the car, I remember having to sit for a while before we drove off. It felt like the whole of my body was on fire right into my eye sockets and I could not see clearly enough to drive. I would have to do that all over again another two times that week and every week for the next nine months!

During this time, and because I had let my health suffer, what would have been hard work became a huge mountain that felt unscalable. Over a period of time I had allowed myself to get so run down to the point of damaging my body as I had not put enough effort into taking care of myself. At this point, I was also unbelievably bad at accepting help. I guess I wanted everyone to think *I had got this*.

I think I had become such a good actress by this point that I even kept the fact that I was struggling physically from my husband, and he knows me best. He was supporting me so much with my mental health and doing so much for our boys, that I did not want to add to it. Telling him was the best thing I could have done. Being in denial about how I was coping did not help. Neither did keeping quiet, ignoring glaringly obvious physical signs, and paying no attention to the frightening thoughts in my head. That was a huge mistake.

I believe that if I had talked to my nearest and dearest and then paid a visit to my doctors in the early days, I would have got the help I needed. When I needed to ramp up the care for one or both of my children, I would have been in a better place to do that.

Seeing my children in pain and not being able to make it better certainly took its toll and at that time I had no idea that stress could cause numerous problems for me and my health if not checked. I should have taken some time to care for myself so that I was in a better condition to care for them.

What do they say? *Apply your own oxygen mask first before you help others with theirs.* How true is that!

When I look back and question why I had ignored these signs, there are a couple of things that come to mind and perhaps you will be familiar with some of these feelings too?

I feel it would be useful at this juncture to share some of the pitfalls I found in the hope you may avoid them. In the next chapter, we will have a look at some of the excuses we can come up with which end in denying ourselves some love too.

CHAPTER 4

I'm Fine, Honestly

I AM A HUGE fan of the band Panic at the Disco and these lyrics to the song 'Always' really resonate with me, *I could kid myself in thinking that I'm fine.*

As human beings we are particularly good at using *I'm fine* as our default answer regardless of how we are feeling, and it is my experience that as parents we are experts. So why do we instinctively close that conversation down?

I have a few ideas and maybe some of these will feel uncomfortably familiar to you too. This is a short list of some of the excuses I feel we may use to convince ourselves that we are indeed fine.

- It's not about me - it's about my kids.
- I really don't have time for any of this.
- I need to distract myself from the truth that I am anything but fine.

- I doubt that if I shared this with anyone they would understand.

I think we need to spend some time unpacking some of this. Let's start with the first excuse on the list and the one I have heard most often.

It's not about me - it's about my kids

I can almost see you nod your head adamantly with regards to this and I would imagine you have never even considered otherwise.

This is a huge one, and I know that every parent who has shared that sentiment with me over the years, has believed it to their very core and each time I hear it, it breaks my heart. This is why I think we believe this and why I think it is so sad.

I believe that when we see our children suffer with their physical and mental health, when that trauma is so hard, relentless, and seemingly never-ending we give up all hope that there will ever be any time for us. We then resign ourselves to that is just the way it is. Right now, I feel really privileged in bringing you a little hope.

You can afford to give yourselves some care and time too.

Here is the icing on that parenting cake

I believe it actually makes us better parent carers and gives us more stamina and strength to run the race ahead.

Having that default of *it's not about me* might just be hard-wired into us as parents. To find evidence for this, we only have to look toward the animal kingdom to see this attitude replicated time and time again. Species such as seals, orangutans, and penguins go to extreme lengths, even to their own detriment to care for their offspring and it seems we are no different. How lucky are we then that we have the intelligence to challenge that and find an even better way of doing things?

Every parent I have ever met has carried some guilt about considering their own well-being, but I really believe that taking time to care for yourself is incredibly healthy and can only be beneficial to your children as well. Perhaps even more than that

I believe we have a duty to our children to look at ourselves!

So now I have addressed that behemoth, let's talk about the other items on the list.

I really don't have time for any of this

You may respond with *"fine"* when someone asks how you are because, in your mind, you are already run off your feet looking after your child. To even entertain the idea that you are not fine, means finding time for yourself, and admitting you are struggling is hard!

However, we have looked at how important it is to take some time to establish your normal. You can be aware when something is not right and know how beneficial it is to do that sooner rather than later. We have also looked at how life can be made even harder when we let things slip.

I have also found this to be true. Regardless of whether we think we have time to deal with any of *this, this* is still happening. We may as well ensure we are in the best possible shape to deal with it. Hopefully, we can be honest with ourselves and accept we need to find the time to care for ourselves too. When we can be honest with ourselves it is so much easier to be honest with others.

We may find we are in a much better place to ask for help and I will go into more details about that later. Now *I don't have time* is off the table – what other lies have we been telling ourselves?

Let's look at the third excuse.

I need to distract myself from the truth that I am anything but fine

In the early days, I was a champion at this, if anyone asked how I was I would reply, *fine thanks.*

For the longest time, this was my go-to reaction whenever anyone broached the subject of my health. When I look back, I went to some impressive lengths to keep up with this façade, you may be familiar with this yourself. Being in denial and then covering it up with something or anything, is a way to cope albeit not a healthy one.

This is an example of how I did this.

I would imagine you have been in that situation when a friend or family member has contacted you to say they are in the area and could they pop in for a cuppa. In the past when that happened, I insisted that the whole family enter into a mission impossible state of mind. We would run around like a headless chicken hoovering, dusting, cleaning, and shoving things in handfuls into cupboards to give the impression that the state of the house mirrored my state of mind. By the time our visitors arrived, I was hot and bothered and had expended a huge amount of energy in a ridiculously small space of time. The daft thing was that anyone I felt comfortable inviting into my home really could not have cared less at the state of our house, they were there to see and support us not marvel at our spotless home. It is all too easy to fall into a trap of wearing ourselves out over nothing.

It is interesting to note that during the difficult years this mindset of keeping up appearances became more apparent and I now know this was one of my ways of distracting myself from real life. When you stop and look at how you cope and deal with difficult situations you may well see a similar pattern. However, you can change your mindset and ensure that you have enough energy to care for your child and have some quality *you* time, whatever that may look like. It may also be useful to remind ourselves that there are both positive and negative distractions as well.

We can see how the negative reaction of working myself into the ground was really bad for my mental and physical well-being However, we have also looked at the flip side and seen how a positive distraction such as Netflix or Land Rover maintenance can be beneficial.

If you are unsure of which you are partaking – ask yourself this question

How does this make me feel?

Most importantly be honest with yourself.

For me tidying the house may have been my way of feeling better but in reality, it was robbing me of the little energy I had. It was right here that I discovered a particularly important lesson.

When you find yourself only running on fumes, leave it, leave everything apart from the basics you need to function.

I appreciate that your form of distraction may be something completely different, but it is worth asking yourself whether you need it and how much energy that distraction is using up?

It may be a useful exercise to just to sit and make a note of what you do in a day. Pay close attention to those things you do to distract yourself and ask yourself if they have a positive impact on you.

So now we have talked a little about the benefit of being aware of where your energies are being directed, let's have a look at the last excuse on the list and I believe this is another big one.

I doubt that if I shared this with anyone they would understand

I have a secret for you, and it is very simply this. In my experience when someone who genuinely cared about me asked how I was, and when I answered honestly, they responded with compassion regardless of whether they understood. That works well because, when I got to that stage, what I needed was compassion. Understanding could come later for me and my loved ones.

I hope that you now understand a little of how and why we hide behind distractions and denial and how it is beneficial to both us and our children to be honest about how we are feeling. But how do we answer that question, *how are you,* when perhaps we are not even sure ourselves.

In the next chapter, we are going to look at how we can learn to understand and describe our own feelings.

CHAPTER 5

How are you?

ASK YOURSELF THIS QUESTION, honestly.

I know this question may sound alien because you are used to people asking how your child is or how you are coping with their illnesses but take time to really ask yourself this question.

But how do you describe how you are feeling if what you are feeling is something you have not experienced before? Perhaps if I share my experience with regards to this it may help.

I remember sitting with my doctor fairly early on in my journey, feeling like a rabbit caught in headlights. At the time I was sleep-deprived and I am sure that you will appreciate how difficult that can make things. At that time, my thoughts were also with my child who I had left with a friend so when she asked, *what can I do for you,* my reply went something like this.

'I am exhausted, and I don't know what to do, my child is very ill' ...... and before I knew it I was sitting there telling my doctor how my children were and once again I had made myself invisible. The doctor responded with the appropriate level of empathy and gently said, 'this is about you, how are you?'

So, I told her the truth.

'I feel sad all of the time. I have trouble shutting off all the white noise in my head. I struggle getting to sleep and if I do, I struggle staying asleep. I cannot concentrate on anything for more than a few minutes. I keep thinking something awful is going to happen. I feel like I am walking uphill in treacle. Everything aches and I feel like my limbs are made of stone. I feel like everybody is looking at me and judging me all the time. I really struggle to leave the house and it has been really difficult coming here today.'

After pouring out my heart, I learnt something valuable in that consultation. Your doctor does not need you to express how you feel in medical language, so don't worry about that. It is far more useful to express how you feel in simple language, and from my experience at the time that was all I was capable of doing.

These days there is a danger with all the information that is available to us now to diagnose ourselves. Biting the bullet and making an appointment with your doctor and having the opportunity to sit opposite someone (albeit virtually at present) and tell them exactly how it is goes a long way to ensuring you get the help you need. Very quickly my doctor picked up what was wrong and set me on a path to improve things.

Going back to the list of things I initially shared with my doctor, I wonder if perhaps some of the feelings I had are familiar to you too? If you are sitting there reading this and there is something that strikes a chord with you, then I would urge you to consider making that appointment now.

There is help available and as we have discussed anything that may make your life as a carer a little easier is worth looking into. The sooner you do that the sooner you may find you are able to cope better.

Also, if any of the words I used to describe my feelings resonate with you, a word to the wise, write them down. You may find it a lot easier to have something to read from when you make that doctor's visit, and you are likely to feel a lot more at ease and less anxious if you have it all there in front of you.

I mentioned that the doctor set me on the right path, and for me that included medication. I just want to chat with you a little bit more about that and share my experience with you, but it is extremely important that you bear the following in mind.

Everyone is different, we all have slightly different metabolisms and different baselines, so it is likely that every individual will respond differently to medication. This is just my experience and if you speak to someone else you are likely to find their experience is different. Firstly, it was not a quick fix, it took about 6 weeks from when I received my prescription for me to notice I was coping better and it kind of crept up on me. I would find myself thinking. *A couple of weeks ago I would not have coped with today's drama nearly as well* or *I have slept right through for the last week. I dealt with that a lot better and my head was a lot clearer.*

I have spoken to many people on this subject and encouraged carers in the past to seek medical help. I have found that their experience albeit different from mine was a positive one. Something else that was also extremely beneficial and was part of my care package was talking therapy.

I know for a lot of people there is still a stigma attached to anti-depressants and talking therapy. Very sadly some feel it is a sign of weakness. However, when you have read about my experience and when your body and mind are coming under such vicious fire, I think even the most sceptic would bite the hand off the person offering that kind of help, especially if it made things easier. The medication and the opportunity to talk to an unbiased professional about how I was feeling has provided a much-needed crutch over the years. If it helps you can look at it like this.

Imagine all your hurt, pain and trauma is like an open infected wound. You can smear some antiseptic cream on it and slap on a plaster hoping that will stop it weeping and getting worse. However, until that wound is cleaned out and cleanly dressed it will not start to heal properly. From experience, the quicker that can be done then the less likely the infection is to spread. If a seriously infected wound is left completely alone it is highly likely that the body will succumb to sepsis, then you are in serious trouble.

I won't ever underestimate how hard it is to take the first steps to get help. Even when a medical professional is dealing with that infected wound and applying their knowledge to dealing with it, it is still going to hurt - a lot. I believe it takes a certain type of courage to walk toward that hurt. I looked at my talking therapy as a means to an end and I only wish I had made that brave step earlier in my journey.

I am really hoping that by the time you get to the end of this chapter, you will at least be starting to consider that how you feel does matter and it is OK to be anything other than *fine*. If that is so you are making some fantastic and brave progress, so at this point, I would love to share with you that fantastic news that you are not on your own.

In the next chapter, we will look at perhaps the most beneficial thing available to you as a parent carer and that is your support network.

CHAPTER 6

Who is Supporting You?

WHO OR WHAT IS your support network? These are the people in your life who provide emotional or practical support.

For a lot of people, the majority of that network are likely to be made up of family and friends. However, support can also be available from other sources, such as medical professionals, charities, teachers, and employers. It has also been my experience that when you are brave enough to be honest about what you are going through, there are all sorts of people you may come into contact with regularly who will respond to that honesty with offers of help too.

I am very aware that not everyone is lucky enough to be surrounded by friends and family, and some may be isolated due to the situation they find themselves in with their children. Even if you find yourself in that position, there are some wonderful online communities that would welcome and support you (you can find some contacts at the back of this book).

To give you an idea, I shall show you the sort of people who rallied around us and how I dealt with making that leap from *I'm fine* to accepting help in whatever form it presented itself.

Honesty with friends and family

I will start this by going right back to basics and sharing with you something which has become a bit of a mantra for both myself and other parents I have worked with in the past.

There is no shame or guilt in accepting that you need help yourself when you are dealing with such extreme circumstances.

The reason I say this with such conviction is because it makes perfect sense. When you are in the middle of your own *disaster* movie it is extremely hard to explain to anyone else what you are going through. The only way they could possibly understand is if you could reach out and pull them in with you. You can describe what is it like to see a volcano erupt but if you were not there you could not feel the ground shaking, the fear, the smell of burning, or the heat on your skin.

Sometimes things felt so surreal to me, that I had no idea how to communicate the feelings to those close to me who needed to know. One of my concerns was that if I could not convey the emotions I was feeling eloquently, how would I be able to reach out and express my need for physical comfort as well as practical help.

The only way for me to express my feelings to those who were closest to me at the time was to remove the emotions and deal in cold hard facts. If I let in the emotion, I could not make it through a sentence. Looking back this would have been a really good time to go back to simple language again and you may find that useful again too.

I could have expressed my feelings in ways such as: -

I am really worried about X.

I am struggling to know what to do.

I think I really need help, but I can't exactly put into words what I need.

I feel like there is no sign of this improving and I just want someone to talk to.

I would not be surprised if another concern you have is *what if they don't get it?*

Let's go straight back to that comforting thought which is, when someone who genuinely cares for you asks how you are and you answer honestly, they are highly likely to respond with compassion regardless of whether they understand. And remember that reaction is really helpful because when you get to that stage what you need is compassion. Understanding can come later. This was absolutely my experience.

It did not matter how coldly I expressed the current state of affairs, the reaction was still the same. I found that those who knew me really did not need an explanation. They did not need to understand or to come up with a fix-it all they wanted to do was wrap me in their arms and let me break for a little while. The practical help could wait.

I can't express how much that meant. It was like putting your fist through a dam wall and letting the force of water break through until there was less power behind. All that was left to do was then wait until it had calmed on the other side. It was in those moments of calm that I could see more clearly, and it was easier to make plans and figure out some of the practical stuff.

I would just like to take you back to my initial appointment with the doctor and how in that moment it was important to focus on how I was feeling and my perspective of the situation.

In my experience, it was the same when I was talking to my nearest and dearest. If they were not confused by tales of what was going on with the children and worrying about how they could help them, it was easier for them to focus on me and my current needs. After all, it was me standing in front of them asking for help and not my child.

Also, and this is a really important point to consider, I was very aware that a lot that was shared with family and close friends often needed to be diluted. It is for the same reason that I have been extremely cautious about what I have shared in this book. I did not want to upset them unnecessarily, but more importantly, there was the question of confidentiality. These people I spoke with knew my children very well and it was important I was aware that my children may not want me to share some things about them. We may have a story to tell but it is also their story and they have a right to choose when and who to tell it to.

Also being in a position where I could express my concerns from my perspective, made it easier to establish how having practical as well as emotional support could benefit us all.

Once I had let the waters subside and calm ensued for a while I could sit with friends and family and figure out what that practical help could look like.

Our parents were amazing and helped out with anything they could, even taking care of our children so we could have a break. We found it was immensely helpful when they were willing to take on some of the more mundane jobs such as housework and shopping too.

Looking at some of the things I found incredibly helpful may give you some ideas.

Housework

As we have established when you are a parent carer and are running on fumes it is incredibly wise to just do the absolute essentials. Having a clean and tidy house was way, way down my to-do list, please consider demoting that too. I was being extremely cautious with what little energy I had, and I found that housework was something that could quite easily be given to those kind people who had offered help. I remember my wonderful sister-in-law who is a force to be reckoned with when it comes to organisation, flying around our house cleaning like a whirlwind, while I just sat completely fazed and slightly perplexed at the whole thing.

We were able to put the washing in black bags and when someone offered assistance, giving them a load of washing to do, was a huge help and they were delighted to do something practical. I will however add here that I did exclude a few items, some things are just above and beyond the call of duty!

Food

I know that I must have responded to offers of help by asking people if they would mind doing a bit of shopping. There were times I was so exhausted I did not even remember this had happened until I opened the cupboard and found it full. It may also have been that some thoughtful person had put it away without asking. It was wonderful to know someone had dealt with that essential need and a great comfort when shopping at times like that was tantamount to conquering Everest.

At other times friends would cook for us so that all we had to do was pop a casserole in the oven. I remember very clearly coming home after a particularly difficult day turning into our drive and seeing a parcel wrapped in one of those old-fashioned checked tea towels that your nan always had. I knew immediately that we had had a visit from one of the lovely older ladies at our church and that we would have a delicious home-cooked food within half an hour. It was probably one of the best meals I have had.

That was invaluable as the thought of cooking after some days was overwhelming and I would have probably gone to bed on a bowl of cereal again. Although I will add here that a bowl of muesli is an excellent source of nutrition if that is all you can manage.

There are other things that were extremely helpful to us too.

During the time I was making numerous weekly hospital trips shortly after my ME diagnosis, a wonderful lady, who was in my life at the time, supported us at every appointment she could. She would pick us up, do all the heavy wheelchair lifting, and it was lovely to have someone to sit and chat with while I was sat in the waiting room.

This was so precious because it meant I had more energy to give to my children when I was at home and I could also do the best I could to resemble a wife.

Perhaps when someone asks you if they can help, you can once again steer away from the now notorious, *I'm fine* and respond a little more appropriately. Also, it was good to ask people to do something I knew they would be comfortable doing. For example, you may know people who love cooking, so you could say; *I would really appreciate one of your lovely home-cooked meals to pop in the freezer for emergencies.*

Or you may know someone who enjoys driving, you could say; *It would be really helpful if you could drive us to this appointment as I need to focus on other things.*

There are even some people out there who actually enjoy ironing, no, honestly, so you know what help you could ask for there.

Utilise them and please be at peace doing that guilt-free because I have another secret for you.

It has been my experience that when friends and family make the offer and ask 'is there is anything we can do' they mean it. And that asking for or accepting help can be immensely helpful and healing to the person offering, as being able to do anything often is a great comfort to them. You are likely to be doing them a favour as well.

There is truly little anyone can do during any sort of illness to make the person better, but what they can do is improve the situation as a whole.

Knowing your Cheerleaders

I have spoken a lot about being aware of the things that are good for us and beneficial to our well-being especially during periods of stress. Unfortunately, with that in mind, you may find you have people in your life who add to the stress instead of helping you bear it.

In the past, I have asked parents to consider whether it would be better if they let some friendships go. This may be something you may like to give some thought to as well.

There may be some who will talk but will not listen. There may be some who seem to have it much worse than you. There may some who will expect you to function at the level you did pre-trauma and perhaps won't understand that you will have neither the resources nor the energy to keep giving at that same level.

Ask yourself, *am I better for spending time with that person?*

If you are reading this and someone comes to mind, the last thing I want to do is heap on any more stress. You do not need to be in a situation where you are in danger of being caught in any conflict, you can let things fade a little more gently.

For example:

Do not be so eager to respond to the message that pops up on social media or the invitation for coffee, after all, you have a lot of genuine excuses as to why you are too busy.

Just remember you need to be careful about how you use the energy you have and unfortunately that may mean you cannot deal with anyone else's dramas.

We have already looked at how important it is to explore where your energies are being directed and that includes considering the people you surround yourself with. Be aware of how you spend your very precious time and energy and ensure that any input you receive from those around you is positive, constructive, and nurturing. I hope you will take some comfort from this.

It has been my experience and I honestly believe that good friends and supportive family will not have any expectations or make any demands on you. They will certainly not think any less of you when you accept and reach out for help.

Never forget, as I have said, this is a symbiotic relationship and by accepting the hand that is offered to you, you are highly likely helping them cope with the situation as well.

I am really hoping that by now you will be feeling a little more comfortable about talking to family and friends and see how beneficial it is to recognise your real cheerleaders.

In the next chapter, we will look at who are the other people who may be part of your wider support network.

CHAPTER 7

Additional Help and Where to Find It

WE HAVE TALKED ABOUT my experiences with relation to my family and close friends but what about the other support that I now know is available. It can be immensely helpful to know what is out there too.

In this chapter, I will share some experiences both myself and my husband have had when dealing with the various crises life threw at us, and I will introduce you to the people who became our everyday heroes.

I hope that this will give you an idea about the other people you can reach out to. I understand how all-consuming caring for a poorly child can be, so I thought I may help if I gave some examples about how we got these people on board.

A lot of parents I have spoken to have not been aware of additional help in their area. They were often too exhausted to even contemplate looking into anything. As crazy as it may seem, I think right from the outset I felt that I am on my own in this, and I would imagine you have had the same sentiment. I remember thinking *if I am lucky enough to get help for my child that would be great but beyond that, I have not given it any thought, especially where support for myself is concerned.*

I mentioned briefly that it was my experience when I started to be honest about what I was going through, that more help was offered from many different sources.

Before I set up my first support group for parents caring for a child with mental health issues, my co-workers and I spent the best part of a year building up a network of people that we could signpost our parents too. This proved to be some of the most beneficial work we have done.

I appreciate that some of the help available is dependent on where you live and it can be a bit of a postcode lottery, but there are a lot of national organisations out there that are geared to support you and your child. I have included a list of outside agencies and charities that you may want to refer to at the end of the book. It is my hope that having the opportunity to signpost you to some of those may help in your journey going forward.

But first, let us look a little closer to home and at some of the sources of help we found. These included employers, teachers, paramedics, and pharmacists and I shall expand a little on each.

These are in no particular order but came to mind when I brainstormed and looked back on our journey. This is how they were beneficial to us and our situation. I appreciate at this point that regardless of what you are dealing with as a parent carer, there will still be bills coming in and the outside world will still expect you to keep functioning as you always have. You will know that when you are struggling with whatever life has thrown at you, that is incredibly difficult.

One of our biggest challenges during the difficult years was finding the energy to continue working. We wanted to ensure that financial difficulties weren't something else we were adding to the plethora of issues and I have spoken to enough parents over the years to recognise this is a huge issue for many others too.

So firstly, I would like to share with you how beneficial it was to find the courage to talk to and be honest with employers and let them have a little window into what you are facing.

Your Employer

I gave up work early on in this process to care for my children, and I remained unemployed until recently.

My husband is the breadwinner and as such during the difficult times, he was under a huge amount of pressure to stay fit enough to continue working. He works for a huge retail company in a responsible job and the support he received from the company during the difficult years was nothing short of excellent.

He was lucky enough to have a boss who would listen, even though he did not fully understand what he was going through. There we are again with the compassion and understanding idea.

His boss dealt with absences and sudden exits from work with grace and empathy and I believe one of the key elements to this understanding was my husband's honesty from day one. He did not sugar coat any of the issues.

When the first problems arose with our children, my husband went to his boss and told him what was going on. Not only did that build up trust it also meant that when he received that urgent panicked phone call from me, he could just drop what he was doing and come home.

He was also honest about how he was managing the current workload. Had all been quiet at home he would have had the energy to carry on working at the capacity he always had. However, his boss recognised that stress and sleepless nights take a heavy toll and looked at ways he could adjust his workload to accommodate that.

You remember what I said about the benefits of making a doctor's appointment. My husband was honest with his GP about how he was coping not just at home but also at work. This is a good example and shows how having an honest relationship with both can really work in your favour.

There were benefits for me too. Being aware of my husband's positive and supportive work situation was a huge comfort. I knew that when he went out to work, he did not have to adopt the *stiff upper lip* which we have explored can be exhausting. There was even a time that we both met with his boss for coffee so that he could reassure me about the measures the business had taken to support us. Looking back, I realise what an absolute blessing that was. Also opening the conversation early avoided the potentially stressful situation of having to explain everything that had happened leading up to that moment.

You may find the idea of sharing the current situation with your employer a little daunting, if so, perhaps the first port of call could be sharing with a trusted colleague. It's often easier to approach this with someone you trust by your side. Again, it may be useful to use simple language just as we discussed when having that first consultation with your doctor. You may find it easier to go to HR first as well and then they will be able to facilitate that meeting with your boss.

Consider the benefits of writing it down. If you struggle knowing how to approach this ask a friend to help you. Also bear in mind that this is about YOU. You can explain in simple terms the situation with your child to set the scene for your employer or HR but don't forget, that as much as I am sure they will react with compassion, they cannot do anything to help your child. They want to know how they can help you.

I'd like to reassure you that even in a work situation you don't have to do this on your own and as mental health affects such a large amount of people today it's likely that anyone you confide in will have had some experience of it, whether personally or someone they know.

My husband has since had the opportunity to speak up and share some of his experiences with others at work. He shared how being honest with his boss and his colleagues had been incredibly beneficial and had ensured he had received the appropriate support. If he hadn't been open, it would have been much harder for us.

Since he spoke up at work there have been a number of occasions when colleagues have approached him for a chat. They had been going through similar situations with their children and had recognised how beneficial it would be to talk to someone who got it. Being able to support or just listen to another person who has identified with you can really help your own healing process too.

How true is the saying *honesty always goes a long way* and it just takes a few of us to take those first steps before things can change. Not only can it make life a little easier for you, but you could also be changing things for the better for that person who comes after you too.

Your GP

We have talked about the benefits of making that early appointment with your doctor and making sure they are aware of your circumstances. You can see how it helped in a work situation when the GP was able to support my husband's case. It has also been my experience that doctors I have seen in recent years have had a lot more understanding about the parent carers role and how it can take its toll on health both mentally and physically.

Our GP has taken the time not just to understand my individual medical needs, but has also treated the family as a whole, recognising the need for holistic support. Get your GP on board and don't be scared about asking for their help with regards to supporting you as you navigate additional help for your children too.

Support at School

This is perhaps one of the most challenging issues I have faced as a parent and it is a really tough one because I have had really mixed experiences with both my children. I have spoken to enough parents to realise I have not been alone in this. Some I've met feel like they are banging their heads against a brick wall, whilst others will tell you they could not wish for better support. And I can only imagine what different scenarios you are going through.

I would like to first share some of my positive experiences with you.

September has always been a difficult time for us. I think it is to do with everything going back to *normal* for so many. Back to college, back to school, back to work after the long summer holiday. For those who struggle and whose life is anything but *normal* it just widens the gap between them and those who cope. It heightens the realisation that they are not able to do what others appear to do so effortlessly.

On one such September, one of our boys was finding that attending school was becoming more and more difficult for him. Surprisingly, in the first week of the new term, I received a phone call and a visit from his head of year. The teacher was keen to put a plan in place to ensure my son received appropriate help going forward. The willingness to help and the compassion he showed my son meant an awful lot in those first few months, the school tried and that is what mattered.

I received the same excellent support in previous years from the staff at my son's primary school. The head encouraged, challenged, and pushed just the right amount and went above and beyond in her role. I was able to be completely honest. Just like my husband with his employer, I did not have to sugar coat the situation and quite honestly if I had rolled up to school pick up still in my pyjamas, she would have got it.

As you can see from these experiences those wonderful teachers showed compassion to my children and to me as a parent. For many of those staff, it was a steep learning curve, but they did what they could to make the learning experience a positive one and that was a huge comfort.

When I dropped off my child in the morning (which I appreciate can often be anything but smooth), I left knowing they were in good hands. I am sure you are familiar with being able to leave your own child at the school gates and have the confidence that they will be fine. This gives you the space and peace to be able to get on with your day and do what you need to do.

Unfortunately, I have also experienced the opposite and I know many of you will be able to identify with some of these issues. Let's have a look at the negative aspect of this and then see how we can find some hope in all of it.

Unlike my previous experience, when seeking support for a child with mental health issues, one particular school did not *get it* and many times I felt like the hysterical mother! I had previously experienced appropriate support for both my child and myself so was able to establish fairly quickly that what was being offered here fell painfully short. They also pushed and challenged but, in a way, that was detrimental to my son.

I guess if those few hours he spent every day in school were in an environment where he could relax enough to learn and where he received the appropriate support it would have been worth it, but the truth was that time was hell on earth for my son.

This was incredibly difficult to deal with as a parent. It goes without saying that seeing your child in that amount of distress is soul-destroying, but more than that, I felt completely lost as this was so different from the level of care I had experienced previously.

Looking back, I wish I had acted sooner to change this situation, but I am sure you can appreciate that when you receive advice from a professional you have a certain amount of faith that they know what they are talking about. We will talk about that a little more in the next few chapters.

You may feel as I did at the time that there is little you can do, after all, if nothing else your child attending school is a legal requirement. And I appreciate this, but, and some may find this to be slightly controversial, but I think there is huge unnecessary pressure on us as parents to ensure our children receive an education at all costs.

I stand by and passionately believe that you and your children's good mental health is far more important.

I believe for some children the school environment can be toxic and this has been backed up by the stories I have heard from many parents over the last few years. We had been struggling without any professional support for many years and there came a point for me when I said enough is enough and I bought in the big guns.

At this point, it is my hope that you are getting support from an outside agency such as CAMHS (Child and Adolescent Mental Health Service) for your child. If not, you can find out a bit more about that at the back of the book, but if you are, you can get them involved in your child's schooling.

It was at a meeting with the school educational officer, the head of the school's special educational needs, and a therapist from CAMHS that I discovered that home tutoring could be made available.

As a parent sometimes we must have full-blown tantrums to get what we need for our children. It should not be that way, but unfortunately, it is. I have come to realise that even though this can be exhausting we have a right to push as hard as we need to get the appropriate results. Pushing that hard was one of those times when the energy I poured into it was absolutely worth it. I was able to remove my child from an environment that was utterly detrimental to his well-being and go down the route of home tutoring.

I was able to get a referral to OOST (Out Of School Tuition) through my son's support worker at CAMHS and once I had persuaded the school that this was the right course of action we were quickly assigned a tutor. She worked with my son for up to 5 hours a week. It perhaps doesn't sound a lot, but when it is on a one-to-one basis that is quite a bit of quality learning.

The school paid for the tuition through OOST, so we did not have any additional financial responsibilities, and as the tutor was trained to work with someone with anxiety my son was able to progress with his studies. I had no idea that this or indeed the option to teach your own children was a thing.

I think that during this time of lockdown many parents have been amazed at the ability to facilitate learning at home so you may feel that either of these could be a viable option for you and your child going forward.

If this has you thinking, then I would recommend you contact the SENDIASS (Special Educational Needs & Disability Information Advice and Support Service). It was formerly known as Parent Partnership Services and it may have a slightly different name depending on where in the country you are based but you can find them easily online (or you can contact the Citizens Advice Bureau for the number). This is a good place to start to discuss your options.

As we decided to go down this route, my son has been able to go on to attend college. He enrolled on a pre-sixteen course which is another alternative to attending school. Not all colleges offer this, but in my experience, it is well worth asking the question when you get to that stage.

In the meantime, I hope you have the experience of finding a teacher who understands and is helping your child and offering support to you as well. As a parent dealing with the issues that you are, you deserve that and there are a lot of amazing teachers out there.

If, however, you feel like you are not being heard, I hope you have a little more peace of mind knowing that there are other ways around this and people you can talk to. Don't forget to ask your GP how they might help support you all as well.

Now we have looked at adding your employer, colleagues GP, teachers, or associated outside agencies for education to your support network, let's look at some of the other sources of help.

Additional Sources of Help

Some of the best advice I have been given with regards to not just medication but holistic support for our family's various health issues have come from our pharmacist. She was there to offer support when I wanted to have more information with regards to medication. Thanks to the advice and information I was given, and my personal experience, I can say with a great deal of confidence that I feel this is an avenue worth pursuing if you feel it may help.

She was instrumental in helping us deal with my children's physical health concerns and supported us as we navigated the complex issues that accompanied those. I found that if I had any additional questions that I had perhaps forgotten to raise with my GP very often my pharmacist could answer them with a lot more detail.

There were even times where, because of the ensuing crisis, we found we had run out of medication and forgotten to order a new prescription she would sort out a couple of pills to tide us over until a prescription came through.

So much stress was avoided because of the care she gave us and because of her vast knowledge of the medications we were all taking at that time, I knew I could rely on any information or advice she gave me.

You can also walk into a pharmacy now and ask for a private consultation and many pharmacists can prescribe medication that in the past could only be authorised by a GP. As their knowledge of medication is often far superior, they can be a huge source of help for you which I would actively encourage you to seek out should you need it.

Paramedics

I know that there have been many parents who will have been in a situation where they have had to call an ambulance for their child after an accident, or when they have become really ill. You may be among them and it is these moments when we are utterly lost that we need someone to gently come in and take control.

We have had paramedics come into our home and carried on calmly with their job and every one of them without exception has acknowledged our distress even though we were not the patient. We have been blessed by these people and honestly believe it takes a special type of person to go into that profession.

I think looking back the best advice I could give you with regards to benefitting from the expertise and knowledge of these amazing people is to take on board what they say. Don't be scared to ask questions, and with regards to the business of self-care, while they are with your child for whatever reason, let them do the caring. Step back for that time, let them do what they need to do, and while that is going on just take a moment to breathe.

These are just a few of the people I have come into contact with who I have considered part of my wider support network and hopefully, you can see how each of these can make a difference to the situation you find yourself in.

Below is a quick re-cap and some more ideas of the sort of help you can tap into. You can also find more details at the back of this book.

- Employer
- HR
- Colleagues
- GP
- Therapist or Counsellor
- Pharmacist
- Teachers
- CAMHS (Child and Adolescent Mental Health Services)

- SENDIASS (Special Educational Needs & Disability Information Advice and Support Service).
- CAP (Christians against Poverty)
- CAB (Citizens Advice Bureau)
- Charities
- Facebook Communities

In more recent years I have relied an awful lot on *to-do* lists. I have used them for everything from shopping to help with packing for holidays and the ones I used in our recent house move filled a couple of notebooks. These lists have proved incredibly helpful time and time again. It struck me how useful that would have been to have all the information we had learnt at hand during the difficult years.

Why not start making a list of your own? This can help when you are in a crisis and need help but cannot think of anyone. This will also help you build confidence in yourself that you do know where to go for help when you need it.

It has often been the folk who are not the most obvious sources of information who have made the most sense. During the course of my journey, I have learnt that the more I read and talk to different knowledgeable people, the more you come across the infuriatingly elusive information that I wish I had known at the time.

I can only share the experience I have had with some of these people and organisations and as we have discovered your experiences will be different as will the help that is available in your locality.

However, the most important thing here is that I hope you do see that you are NOT on your own in all of this. No matter what your current circumstances are there are people, kind compassionate people who are willing and qualified to help you.

It is incredibly beneficial to understand who you can enlist into your support network and how having that list with your contacts close at hand could be a huge help. So now you have some more knowledge and people onboard who you trust, we can start looking at some of the tougher aspects of being a parent carer.

For me and many other parents, I have spoken to in the past, one of the biggest obstacles and stumbling blocks were the dreaded appointments. Those appointments we find we must attend both to get into the system and once we are in it.

In the next chapter, we will look at how we can survive and thrive in those appointments. We will also look at why I have realised that asking the right questions and having the right person by your side are possibly two of the most powerful weapons in a parent's arsenal when dealing with this.

CHAPTER 8

Help Dealing
with
Appointments

WHEN I WAS BRAINSTORMING ideas for the *things
I know now I wish I knew then* I realised that one of
the most difficult things I had to deal with was
surviving appointments.

There was always the worry that I would forget
important things I wanted to ask or would miss
something important that I was told.

We all know how long it can take to get a face to
face with a medical professional and I understand
the stress that comes from making sure we milk
them for every drop of useful information and
support we can. So, in the time-honoured fashion of

the great makeover, let's have a look at the *before* and *after*.

First, I will share with you an absolute train wreck of an appointment I attended, and then we can look at how we can remove the angst and worry in the hope I can help set you up to be prepared and confident going forward.

The Before

As a parent at the end of their tether and doing yet another excellent impression of a rabbit caught in headlights, I sat in a chair while a medical professional fired lots of long and impossible sounding names of medications at me. He may just as well be talking in some alien language because nothing was going in. In that office at that very moment, I would have done anything for that person sitting opposite me. As far as I was concerned, if they had the power to help my child, then what they were offering was pure gold. I just wanted it to be over and for the doctor to hand me the magic prescription slip so we could get out of there before my child started to get really distressed. Right at that moment, they were like a God and I would not have dared question anything they said.

I was broken from sleepless nights and turbulent days and my self-respect and confidence were in tatters. I left with a very distressed child, none the wiser, and with the worry that I had agreed to things with regards to his care that I had no useful information about. I was also aware that after dealing with any fall-out with my child from the stress of the appointment any information that I was desperately trying to hold onto my tired brain was likely to have been deleted.

When later in the evening the tears came, I did not know whether they were tears of anger or sadness or regret or frustration or perhaps all of them. I just knew that I would need to change things so that the fiasco did not happen again.

I am sure that as a parent carer, you are likely to have experienced a similar situation. When you have had to go to some appointment, and after speaking to parents one of the hardest for them had been a mental health assessment. There is such pressure on us as parents to get the questions we are asked or the ones we want to ask right.

Have you been in that position?

Those questions could well be part of what dictates your child's care plan. When you are in that situation when your child is with you there is this frantic multi-tasking going on. You are desperately trying to answer the questions that are being fired at you to the best of your ability while at the same time trying to manage your child's feelings and behaviour.

It is highly likely that you have spent considerable time and effort, no, strike that, blood sweat, and tears to get to where you are right now, and it may just be the nearest you have come to get some practical help for your child.

In those moments it would be useful if we could just split ourselves in half. Half can concentrate on ensuring our child is ok, the other half can listen intently to the person sitting in front of us in the hope there may be a nugget of information that changes everything.

Here is another bit of GOOD NEWS for you: *through trial and error I think I have come up with a better way to do this.*

The After

Firstly, I would have looked at my support network and asked one of those trusted people to come along to all of my son's appointments to act as an advocate. You remember what I said about believing that a good support network is one of your most effective weapons when you are fighting for care, well, these are the moments when support like this can be invaluable.

I have been on both sides of this, benefiting from having that moral support at meetings and being that moral support. Let's have a look at why I feel it works so well.

That person who is with you could do the following: -

Take Notes

As we have discussed when you are sitting in front of that professional at the appointment you have likely waited months for it can be extremely daunting.

When your mind is likely mostly with your child, even if you have left them in good hands it is exceedingly difficult to take things in. You are trying to remember everything that person is saying and you will appreciate what they could be saying may be especially important.

In my experience when I had someone sitting there taking notes it was a huge relief. I was able to relax a little and it was easier to concentrate.

Please take comfort that in that situation, if all you are able to do is sit there and represent your child that is enough.

Ask Questions or Clarify Points

The person who is with you can also ask for confirmation or request more information. They are likely to be a little more distant from the situation and sometimes that makes it easier to concentrate on what is being said.

They could interject with:-

Let me get this straight, this is what you are saying?

Or

Could you explain that again with reference to this situation?

Or

I think X might want another opinion on this, how do I go about it?

I am sure you get the idea.

Answering and Asking Questions

I am sure we have all had that experience, when we have been in a conversation with someone and they ask the question, *is there anything you want to ask me?* I don't know about you, but at that moment, my brain goes blank or diverts straight to *what are we having for tea tonight?*

This is another opportunity for your advocate to step in to ask those questions that may have entered your head and then just as quickly left. Again, join heads with your trusted advocate before the meeting and think of some questions that may be appropriate, and write them down. By the time you get to the end of a meeting, you may feel utterly drained, so you could just hand over that piece of paper and take a moment to breathe.

Be a Spare Pair of Hands

It is very likely that you will be required to attend a lot of these meetings with your child. Your advocate could also be there to continue with the appointment should you need to leave for any reason.

There have been times when one of my children have been too distressed to stay in an appointment because the situation was just too stressful for them.

Help you Prepare for the Meeting or Appointment

Again, this is the beauty of having someone who is slightly distanced from the situation. They are likely to be able to think more practically and could help you write down a few questions you could ask and generally help you prepare. There we go again with the power of writing things down. Just as being in front of your doctor or employer, having something written down when you are attending an appointment can be just as valuable.

Personal Taxi

Ask someone to drive or give you a lift. Not only is this something practical remember you are helping them too. It's one less thing for you to think about and let's face it, some of the car parks at hospitals can cause our stress levels to go up before we have even entered the building.

Also, there have been those valuable moments when I have been able to debrief on the journey home so that I was in the position of still having some energy left once the ordeal was over.

Hopefully, you can see how having a right-hand man or woman there as moral support, scribe, driver, and that extra pair of hands can make the appointment that more bearable.

There are also some things you can do yourself to prepare.

It may sound silly but consider how you dress. Putting on something a little smarter that you feel comfortable in can boost your confidence and self-esteem. You are likely to get a better response from the person you are meeting with than if you turned up in scruffy joggers.

Create your own version of *power dressing*. Also, never forget you know your child best and trust yourself in that.

As a mum, I have had to get to the stage where I have been able to forgive myself for being so clueless at that meeting and wished I had questioned the advice at the time. I wished I had spoken to my pharmacist. I wished I had googled a respectable website such as NHS. I wished I had asked for time to think of questions and wished I had taken along an advocate to support me and that someone had given me that extra confidence and the balls to ask for more time to get advice from other professional sources.

I believe we should be as involved as much as we need to when it comes to care packages, diagnosis, medication, and anything else which impacts our children's well-being.

I hope you can see the value in having a *right-hand* man or woman by your side and that if you spend a little time in preparation it can go a long way to ensure you can get the most out of these appointments.

Please consider this fact. Even though you may feel a bit intimidated by the professional sitting in front of you, if they were really able to acknowledge and understand what a complicated, physically, and mentally harrowing job you are doing, quite frankly they should feel a little in awe of you!

It is not just situations with regards to health that we have a right to be involved in or question. We have a right to fight for the way our children are treated, respected, and accepted.

In the next chapter, I would like to share a story and some of my experience that highlights the importance of this and to bring you some hope that all the blood sweat and tears we expend are sometimes utterly worth it.

CHAPTER 9

Dealing with Authority

IN THIS CHAPTER, WE will look at the benefits of challenging unacceptable behaviour with regards to how our children are treated and how when we approach this with confidence. This can lead to validation for both ourselves and them. I would like to illustrate this by sharing a story with you.

One afternoon my son was sat with some friends when they were surrounded by about fifteen students from the same school they attended.

I have learnt that children can be very cruel to each other, and because my son was, in their eyes, a minority, I would imagine they thought he was ideal victim material. These bullies made hideous threats relating to him and me. They then proceeded to throw stones at the terrified group and threatened to beat them with some metal pipes they had found.

I am sure you will be able to relate to that extremely specific brand of anger you feel when your child is hurt, especially when it is not an accident and especially at the hand of bullies.

I am not proud to say I thought about rounding them up and drop-kicking them off a large cliff. It seemed a fair reprisal after what they had put my child through! However, my anger gave way to focusing my energies on getting some justice for what my son had been through. I felt very strongly that the perpetrators should not feel that they could treat another human being the way they had and get away with it.

I thought my obvious port of call would be the school the bullies attended, but unfortunately because the incident had happened out of school hours and not on school property, to some extent their hands were tied. I felt extremely disappointed and was very distressed at what I perceived was a lack of care. I still felt angry with them because I felt my son was not getting enough support from them, so I guess this made me even more determined to get some sort of justice.

I rang my friend, a parent with a child the same age and a solid member of my support network, as I wanted some reassurance that my anger was justified. I also thought it would be beneficial to talk through some options and together we concluded that this incident was serious enough to get the police involved.

I phoned the police and explained the situation. Their response was what I was hoping for and the following day I went along with my son and three other young people to support them as they gave their statements to the police.

The officer we saw asked lots of questions and was very patient. The four young people involved bravely gave statements and answered questions. Thanks to their willingness to co-operate their statements were signed off and filed. To be honest I did not expect any more to come of it.

A few days later my son and I received a visit from our neighbourhood policeman. It was a meeting that had a profound effect on us both. This policeman was a credit to his profession.

He was disgusted at what had happened and when he had read the statements, he elevated the accusation of bullying to "hate crime" and assured us he was taking it very seriously.

A little more than a week later, I received a call from him with an update. He said he had spoken to the main five instigators with their parents and threatened that if they so much as looked at my son in a threatening way, he would have them arrested. He said that he felt that all those parents present were quite capable of finding a suitable punishment for their children and that they had been horrified at their actions. He asked whether it was alright that he had not carted them off to prison.

I have no doubt that some of the parents would have made those kids' lives a misery for a while as I have no doubt that others would probably not have done a great deal. That did not matter.

I realised at that moment that when it came to defending my son, I was prepared to cause as much trouble as it took to find someone who was prepared to listen, take action, and ensure he felt validated.

As parents, some of the situations we face that involve our children can be a little daunting. Sometimes there are situations where we feel it is appropriate to get outside agencies or authorities involved. The prospect of what is to follow once you set those wheels in motion can be a bit overwhelming.

I hope you never find yourself in a situation like the one I have shared with you but if you do, I think it is absolutely right and healthy to feel anger.

However, I would recommend you take that anger and use it to focus on figuring out how to get the appropriate help and support, even if that means doing something as serious as contacting the authorities. Please remember that no-one knows your child like you do and therefore you are the only one who really knows what they need. Trust yourself in all of this.

To sum it up, when it comes to facing a fight to get justice and validation get your support person on board and recognise that you are doing a brilliant and extremely hard job. Take a deep breath and be confident in your actions, because when it comes to your child you have every right to be a rottweiler.

Also know that you are entitled to be given the time and consideration to ask questions, fight for the right support, and, if you want to, challenge everything.

We have been through so much together in this first section. We have looked at how we can determine if we need additional help and how to tackle that. How important and beneficial it is to get your support network up and running and how to navigate some of the obstacles and requirements that come alongside looking after a child with mental and physical health concerns.

I also really hope you feel a little more inspired with regards to the business of self-care and that you are ready to start entertaining that practising this is worth a shot.

With that in mind, in the next chapter, let's explore some of the practical ideas around self-care, and the things we can do to improve our well-being. These ideas may help us feel better and more able to cope as carers.

CHAPTER 10

Practical Ways to Deal with Self-Care

HOPEFULLY, YOU ARE NOW a little more aware of *your normal* no matter what stage you are at on your journey. I trust that you have started to build a good strong nurturing support network and that your first aid kit is accessible.

Start by taking a deep breath and let us enjoy exploring some practical ideas to administer some self-care. Let the pampering commence, 100% guilt-free.

I know it is not an easy thing to do when all your energies and thoughts are with your child, but I just want to stress once more how important it is.

Don't beat yourself up if you don't get this straight away. Any change takes time, you just have to practice a little.

First, I thought it may be useful to ensure that the foundations to understanding the importance of self-care are firmly in place. To do that, I am going to enlist the help of the 5 W's - the Why, Where, Who, What and When.

Why

Simply and because as the famous shampoo commercial says, *YOU are worth it.*

If you have sat on a plane on the runway, waiting for take-off, you will remember the often painful wait as the poor steward or stewardess, who is likely to have drawn the short straw, has to go through all the safety regulations. Perhaps the most important thing they will say is: -

If the sign comes on and the oxygen mask drops down, make sure you apply yours first before helping someone with theirs.

Essential and sound advice. After all, you are not going to be of any use to anyone if you are just about passing out from lack of oxygen yourself.

As a carer, when we first take steps to care for ourselves, we are in a much better place to care for others.

You now know that if you are completely drained, your cup is completely empty and you are running on fumes, caring for your child is unbelievably hard. You also run the risk of completely breaking down, as I did all those years ago.

If you get to that stage where you feel the pressure is building up and you are tempted to ignore your body and become invisible again, just pop the oxygen mask scenario into the top of your first aid kit.

This is something I still reach for now, and if you use it as one of your mantras, I promise it will stand you in good stead for anything you may face in the future.

Where?

Quite honestly that can be wherever you are. I have spent quite a few nights on one of those notoriously uncomfortable chairs that they put next to hospital beds.

Taking into consideration what my Fibromyalgia specialist had said about correct posture and making sure I relaxed when I was sitting down, made me conscious about the unnecessary strain I could have been putting my body under.

There were a number of times my husband grabbed my pillows from home. If I were going to be there for a while at least I could be a bit more comfortable and ensure I did not have to deal with unnecessary aches and pains later. It sounds a little bonkers when I write this now, but that little bit of awareness made quite a bit of difference, and as I am sure you will know and appreciate, you learn to be quite creative.

For some, the *where* may be outside of your four walls. If you can get out and about for a little while, this may be beneficial. During lockdown and when we were living in such strange times, my *where* was walking around a pond a short distance from the house and just taking in some nature.

In the past and when it was not as easy to get out, I found that having a soak in the bath was some *me-time* that was extremely beneficial. The rest of the household knew that unless someone's limb was hanging on by a sinew or Tom Hardy was at the door it was very much in their own interest not to disturb me. Do not feel guilty about keeping that door shut!

I think a *where* can quite frankly be anywhere you can find some peace and solace.

Where is your *where* place?

Make a note to add this to your first aid kit and if at all possible, make sure you visit it as often as you can.

Who?

Hopefully, by now, you will be a little more comfortable and feel a little more at ease about asking for help. As we have already established, it is good to have a support network and people that you may be able to call upon.

If you have started to compile one, don't forget to refer to that list of useful contacts.

If you are in a position where you can leave the house, call up the friend you can dive into a latte with or take up that offer to use the shoulder and ear of your nearest and dearest. Have a good rant.

If you are in a position of being on your own and therefore are somewhat isolated then my heart goes out to you, but I would encourage you to join an online group. I have included a list of helpful sites and charities to consider at the end of this book.

Don't forget as I said earlier, choose your *"who"* carefully and make sure they are supportive. This is precious free time for you, and it is so important that you get as much benefit from it as you can.

Spend time with those people who you feel better for spending time with.

What?

It can be anything that helps with relaxation and offers the opportunity to perhaps zone out for a little while. With that in mind, I would like to introduce the idea of a comfort box.

This is something you can put together as a source of activities you can do with regards to taking some time out. We will look at creating one for you and then in Chapter 14, I will give you some ideas as to how you can set one up for your child as well.

I think it may be my age and it is something I used to tease my Dad about, but I now have *my seat*, the one I always sit in. The one if anyone else sits in will feel strangely uncomfortable due to the death stare they receive. Anyway, by the side of my seat, I have my comfort box.

My comfort box is a basket and contains the following: -

- Notebook - this can be brilliant for those little niggling thoughts and once again there is power in writing things down. I find that if I do it goes a long way to ensuring those thoughts don't become bigger than they need to be. If nothing else it creates just a little more space in your head and helps avoid those annoying scenarios when you waste energy trying to remember the thing you know you should not forget.

- An adult colouring book and some pencils. Quite frankly this is a great idea and honestly one I am really annoyed I did not patent. Sometimes I find that I need to do more than just one thing when I have a busy head. Having something to do with my hands while the TV is on is just something that has worked for me, but we are all different and some of us prefer peace.

  Colouring in can be therapeutic and it can help our thoughts just flow in and out without having to pay much attention to them. You may have other creative outlets and they are incredibly beneficial and healing. When you just want something, you can pick it up quickly this is an ideal activity because it does not require any thought or energy setting up.

- A book – something that I am really enjoying reading at the moment.

  As much as I love my NETFLIX, it is my opinion that there is nothing better than curling up with some great fiction. You notice I say fiction, I find that I don't have to think so much when I am reading a story, but again we are all different and for some, they may find they can drift away reading about facts and figures – whatever works for you.

- My laptop - so that when inspiration strikes, I can sign in and write, something I find incredibly enjoyable and fulfilling.

What would be in yours?

Perhaps when you have a bit of time you could pop one together so that when you get that chance to sit down and relax you can make it as beneficial and enjoyable as possible.

I am sure you can think of some other ideas, and I am sure every comfort box would look quite different. Regardless of the contents, having what you use to aid relaxation on hand also means you don't have to waste energy thinking about what to do and then faffing around finding the things to do it with.

With that in mind, we will look a little more at some of the benefits of managing energy in Chapter 12.

When?

As you will probably know by now, we may have to be a little creative about the when. It may be those quiet moments you have while your child sleeps. You may also find a little peace when your child is being cared for by someone else, and you may only have time to take a few deep breaths. However long you have and wherever you are, try and make those precious moments count.

If it is possible in your current situation, go as far as to book some time in for yourself and be protective of that time.

A tip here: you can give others the incentive to let you have some *me-time* by assuring them they will be better off if you are allowed those moments to properly relax and unwind. Quite simply, when dealing with the *when*, practice self-care as often as you can, and at any moment the circumstances around you allows. Apply liberally, so to speak.

Now we have looked at the 5 W's, it is also interesting to see that there are different areas that we can concentrate on.

According to the many books I have read and the research I did for our parent meetings, there are three main elements of self-care and these cover your physical, mental, and emotional well-being. Although you could also add, pleasure, sensory, social, and spiritual.

As a start, it is probably easier to focus on the first three main elements and I have given a brief explanation of each.

I have also included a few ideas and examples of practical things you could do to address each of them.

Physical Self-care

I would put myself into the category of fit(ish). I believe the definition of this is; fit(ish); semi-fit; kinda fit; and somebody who likes the idea of being fit but equally likes food. Joking aside, I think this is quite a difficult one.

There is so much emphasis on keeping fit and the benefits of exercise, that when we are up to our necks dealing with cantankerous toddlers or teenage angst it can feel like an additional pressure.

However, it has been my experience that the effort of hoisting myself off the sofa to go for that walk has always been worth it. Even if it were just a brisk 10-minute stroll around the block because that is all the time I could spare.

When the opportunity has presented itself, it has also been greatly beneficial for me and my children to get out in the fresh air. Our family loves the outdoors, our beloved Land Rover and roof tent (google it, they're brilliant!) bears witness to this. During the years we have spent hours and hours outside digging in the mud or hunting for fairies or playing with the dog. There is something about being outside, especially in the middle of nowhere, that can be incredibly grounding and comforting.

I am sure you appreciate the notion that sometimes we must consider giving our children what they need rather than what they want. There have been times when I have used bribery to get them outside because regardless of the protests and moaning, I knew, in the long run, it would help. Add in a mini beast hunt, and before I knew it, I found I was enjoying some quality time with them.

For me physical self-care is about doing something in those precious free moments, even if it is just making an effort to get back to the simple things, like stretching, dancing, walking, or finding some peace in the outdoors. More importantly, feeling the benefits and feeling good about it. Here are some ideas to get you started: -

- Dance to your favourite song, upbeat ones are the best. For me, pretty much any song from Queen would cover that. Dance it out and if the kids want to join in all the better. If you are on your own, dance like no one is watching. Once your heart starts beating so you can hear it, you know you are doing some good just getting the blood pumping around your body.

- Do some stretching exercises (YouTube offers some step-by-step simple ones) even if it is just from sitting in a chair.

- Take your breakfast or coffee outside if it is a nice day, the earlier the better. Having a few moments in the morning, when the rest of the house is quiet, just listening to birdsong or the sound of the world waking up around you can enhance mood and give you a great start to the day. You may cringe when I mentioned early but having a slow early start with time and space for you to think about the day ahead has huge benefits that last all day long.

- Go up and down the stairs two or three times, but remember, you don't want to exhaust yourself all in one go. Find a pace that gets your heart beating but suits you and your physical limitations.

- Have a 20-minute nap, or even better, if circumstances allow an early night. You could listen to some soothing music or an audiobook to help you drift off.

- It is also good to get into a routine of waking up early and going to bed early to give yourself the best possible chance of a good night's sleep.

None of these are hard or fast rules. They are just things I have come across, tried, or other people have told me have been successful. I am sure you will find your own ideas that fit in with your lifestyle.

Why not start a list of all the things you could do?

Mental Self-care

I feel that this is probably the most important of all the self-care areas.

You may be looking for a little peace and/or recuperation, or perhaps, on the other side of the coin, something to inspire or motivate. Either way, it is essential to maintain our mood by keeping our brains and thought processes fixed on helpful positive ideas. Not only does this affect how we are feeling but it has far-reaching consequences for our physical health too.

We are bombarded in the news by the continuous stories of hatred, adversity, and crimes. Currently, we are all in the midst of a pandemic and as such we are being bombarded with difficult images and stories.

On top of everything, we may also be dealing with dramas within our own four walls, and the negative thoughts associated with that, so it can help to make a point of surrounding yourself with the absolute opposite.

Where you have the control, surround yourself with positive vibes.

Here are some ideas you could try to ensure you are looking after yourself mentally as well as physically. You could try some of the following and I am sure you can think of some ideas that would be beneficial and that you can tailor to suit your own situation.

- Learn to say NO guilt-free. Take the word *should* from your vocabulary and remember to spend time with those people that you feel better for spending time with.

- Find a new hobby or revisit one that you used to love doing.

- Start a journal. This is a great way of being able to de-clutter your head and get some of those stray thoughts down on paper. I have included some more ideas about how this may be beneficial to both you and your child in Chapter 14.

- Do a bit of de-cluttering. There is a lot to be said about the *Marie Kondo* way of doing things. If you have never heard of her, I recommend a bit of research.

- Re-read one of your favourite books. As I have said as much as I love my hospital and crime dramas there is still nothing like curling up with a good book.

- Learn something new. Read a new book or watch some podcasts relevant to a topic you are interested in.

Is there something you have always been fascinated by? Why not enjoy learning a little more about it?

Don't forget to add your favourites to this list and remember to look after your mental health. As I've mentioned before, it is important to your child's well-being too.

I have tried all the above and have found inspiration, motivation, and at times a much-needed boost.

Emotional Self-care

I believe this is mainly about dealing with the here and now and what is going on in real-time. When we are dealing with trauma, our emotions will fluctuate a lot more than when we are just going through the motions of a fairly normal life.

I have found that it has not been helpful to label an emotion as simply good or bad. More importantly, it is more beneficial just to recognise them as emotions and be at peace with that.

If we can accept that we are feeling a certain way, and go with that emotion, it goes a long way to removing the fear from the situation.

In my experience, changing the way I thought about things and bringing more positivity into my thoughts was another game-changer. But be patient with yourself because effectively you are breaking a habit of a lifetime.

The good news is that amazingly enough, it may only take 21 days to break a habit, and that feels achievable, especially if you can see the benefits straight away.

The only thing you have control over is your own actions and that can really affect how you may feel as well. Remember even when chaos reigns around us, how we behave in that moment can make a huge difference.

To explain that a little more, let's take the scenario of a traffic jam.

What is going on around you is totally out of your control. You could either get really flustered and swear at the traffic and the inconvenience, wishing really unpleasant things on those drivers who sneak down the outside lane trying to jump the queue at the last minute (oh yes, a big pet hate of mine).

Or

You could tell yourself there is absolutely nothing I can do about this, make yourself as comfortable as you can, pop on some favourite tunes, and just let the world do its stuff around you.

I guarantee that whatever faces you at the end of your journey you are likely to get to your destination in a much better state of mind than some of the other drivers who have been queue jumping and trying to control the situation around them.

If you can just practice positioning yourself in the mindset of:

*I cannot do anything to control the environment,
but I can be aware of how I am acting with regards
to caring for myself.*

You may well find that those *traffic jams* suddenly become a lot less of an obstacle.

To this end, and to help you practice here are some of my tips: -

Acknowledge what you can be grateful for

One of the exercises I was given when I was very poorly and not capable of doing much, was to write one thing down at the end of every day that I was grateful for. Amid depression, that was no easy task, so I started with the very basics.

It may have been something as simple as a cup of tea that someone had made for me or hearing a kind word. The very fact that I was looking for these things so that I could present my homework to my therapist that following week, meant that I started to notice a lot more.

Before long, it was not hard to think of three things at the end of the day.

The next step was every morning to write down something I was looking forward to in the day ahead and it was amazing how empowering this was. Start small, keep it simple and don't force it.

This is also a great opportunity to start a journal. All you need is a notebook, a pen, and some coloured pencils or pens (avoid felt tips as I have found they tend to soak through the page). Then just let your creativity flow. Perhaps you could start by writing down some of those things you are grateful for. You could have a page dedicated to a list of the books you want to read or the films you want to watch or maybe your own version of a bucket list. I have found journaling extremely therapeutic and if you want more information there are some great websites and blogs dedicated to this.

Tap into your creative side

Let your ideas flow. That's when your notebook or sketchbook right by where you sit comes into its own.

Take some time and pamper yourself

This could be a manicure or a long soak in the bath. Or (this is one of my personal favourites) you could even go as far as to popping your pyjamas in the tumble dryer or over the radiator, so they are warm when you get into them. Pure bliss!

Do one thing that makes you happy

Write a list of what makes you happy.

Everyone is different but some ideas could be baking, exercising or doing something creative. If you don't have a lot of time, you could refer to your comfort box or just sit and watch an episode of your favourite show.

Hopefully, you can see how such a simple idea can ensure you make the most out of those precious spare moments. You could even incorporate them into your routine if you enjoy cooking or driving or walking with your family, whatever helps you relax.

Spend some time just for you

Try some deep breathing or mindfulness. This can be helpful. My husband found this and still finds it a good practice to help ground him and give him a few minutes space to take stock. I have put some links at the end of this book to help you.

Have a good cry!

It is a fact that a good cathartic cry can be incredibly healing and liberating. Sometimes when we are dealing with all that comes with caring for a child with health issues, we are so overcome with emotions and tiredness that we are too exhausted to cry.

Sometimes we need a catalyst to help with the much-needed release, so watch a sad movie and just go with it when the floodgates open. Don't analyse too much, just cry. Sometimes there is no particular reason, you just need to release your emotions.

I am not suggesting that we throw ourselves a pity party. I am just suggesting from my experience that sometimes it is healthy to let it out.

Do you remember what I said about that dam wall bursting? It is really important to understand that no one expects you to maintain a *stiff upper lip*.

I appreciate that sometimes as parents we must hold it in. There certainly are times that we would feel worse for letting out our emotions in front of our children. But there are also moments, really healing moments when we can cry with them too. Give yourself some compassion for those times when crying feels like the right thing to do.

Try and remember that self-care is essential for your psychological well-being (much like chocolate) and that as such:

You will find the greatest benefit from any activity if you deliberately give yourself permission to do it GUILT FREE.

You will reap the benefits of being a little bit more at peace with yourself and the world.

I would imagine that by now your well-being first aid kit may well be full to overflowing. You have the comfort and feel a little more positive that there are some accessible practical things you can do to make navigating your journey that little bit easier.

I hope you are in a better frame of mind and maybe feeling a little bit re-energised. Let's now have a chat about something that is incredibly important to the parent carer. Having something practical I could do for my child has always bought me a special type of peace and I would imagine you are no different.

I appreciate how hard it is to see your child struggle and feel there is nothing we can do to fix it. We have already established that there is no Haynes manual to help us, neither is there is a magic wand we can wave to make them better.

However, and just as our friends and family can do this for us, we are able to do things to improve the situation as a whole for our children.

In the next chapter, I will give you some ideas as to how you can tap into that, and explore some practical ideas that may be of help to both you and your child.

SECTION 2

Our Child's Well-Being First Aid Kit

YOU HAVE BEEN PARTY to a little of what my child has had to face, and just like numerous parents, I have spoken to I am sure that you will have a whole lot of stories relating to the issues and challenges that are part and parcel of your child's everyday life.

This next section is dedicated to your children. We will explore some of the things that may be anxiety-provoking and how we can manage expectations and energy levels.

Just as I did for your first aid kit, I have also included some tips and tricks of things you could try to help them when they are struggling.

I thought it would be useful to start by looking a little into what may be going on in their heads.

In the next chapter, I hope to give you a little window into some of their thought processes (a peek into their world if you will) and equip you with some knowledge of what they may be dealing with silently.

CHAPTER 11

What's Bugging our Kids?

RIGHT AT THE BEGINNING of this section, I mentioned about giving you a little insight into what might be going on in your child's head. In these next few chapters, we will have a closer look at that and, more importantly, see what I can offer in the form of support.

Having some tools to help my children made a little more sense of the world has bought me a great deal of comfort. I hope it will do the same for you.

In the 80s, Steven Spielberg brought us some great movies. One of my favourites was called 'Inner Space'. If you have not seen it, this is the plot in a nutshell. A down-on-his-luck naval aviator resigns his commission and volunteers for a secret miniaturization experiment. He is placed in a submersible pod and both are shrunk to microscopic size. They are transferred into a syringe to be injected into a rabbit, but the lab is attacked by a rival organization and during a scuffle, he is accidentally injected into a rather hapless human instead. Great family fun and a recommended watch.

Imagine being able to be injected into your child's head. What a confusing and terrifying place that must be. I think as a parent we would jump at the chance if we were able to get some answers as to what was going on in there. Even if it gave us just the tiniest inkling of how to help them.

I have some information and I want to assure you that this did not involve any shrinkage, crystal balls, or mind reading. I just have the privilege of having wonderful children who actually talk to me. Here is some assurance for you if you are a parent of a child, especially a teenager who currently only speaks in grunts: they will eventually progress to full sentences.

That was just a bit of fun, but in all seriousness, I have often said that I would not want to be a young person in today's society in the 21st Century for all the money in the world. Life seems so hard for our kids. Growing up has always been tough and I am sure there were some things you struggled with as a young person.

If we think of any of those things and then add navigating gender, managing social media, and conforming to some of society's impossible goals to name but a few. We can see how these additional pressures our children have heaped upon them can sometimes be crippling.

We may think that our young people go around with their eyes constantly surgically attached to their various devices and completely oblivious to all around them, but I believe this could not be further from the truth.

I have sat down and had numerous chats with my sons, it appears that our young people have a lot on their mind, and it is serious stuff. Sometimes the stuff of nightmares, and often things that no-one of that age should have to be worrying about. I think if we asked our anxious teens what they were thinking about and they gave an honest reply, we might be a little floored by the answer.

I asked my son, and these are just a few of the things that plague his mind.

He worries about all the social injustice in the world, the serious issues around black lives matter, gender discrimination, bullying, and the negative side of social media. He worries about the fact that 150-200 species of plant, insect, bird, and mammal become extinct every 24 hours and about the fact that over 7,200 square miles of the Brazilian rainforest have burned, and as you are reading this it is still burning, and if that continues then the battle to reverse climate change would be lost.

They worry that all this devastation has been caused by past generations doing an appalling job of caring for the planet and that those people in power do not care nearly as much as they should.

It goes without saying that in our current predicament with Covid-19, along with all the changes, comes a whole plethora of new concerns and anxieties.

Recently I was asked if I would share a little about what it is like to be a parent of a child who has mental health issues during this time of lockdown. Stories from around 1,500 parents were shared from all over the country, analysed by Oxford University, and then published in an article in the Guardian. Here are just a few of the statistics.

'As many as one in five primary age children are afraid to leave their homes and are worried there will not be enough food to eat during the course of the Covid-19 outbreak, according to the findings of a survey.'

'Older children are worried about their families, with two out of five (41%) frightened that friends and relatives will catch the disease; just over a fifth (22%) are worried they will catch Covid-19 themselves and one in 10 (11%) are anxious they could pass the infection to someone else'.

Some of you may be finding that during this time your child is coping relatively well.

From speaking to my son, his anxiety has gone down, as he has is not having to face the social challenges he would normally deal with on a day-to-day basis. He is also not having to cope with public transport or college or exams, or the fear that today he may have to deal with something or someone he is not familiar with. He likes his own space and spending time in a safe place, and he enjoys spending time with us and for that, we are extremely thankful.

But on the flip side, understandably, he is very anxious about not seeing his friends and families so much, and he worries a lot about them.

The other huge looming issue is re-integration. I have spoken with other parents recently with regards to this, so I would not be surprised if this is a current issue you may be facing with your child at this time too.

The main concerns are:-

- How is the world going to work now?
- How am I going to cope with all the changes?

I am concerned that when the time comes there will be many young people who will need a lot of support with this going forward. For some of you, this time will be even more challenging. If you are not a key worker, you will have your children at home *all* of the time.

I have worked with many students over the years, most of who have ASD and related issues. Every one of those students were a delight, and they all had their own wonderful personalities. However, it has been challenging work, sometimes very physical, and many times I returned from work feeling mentally and physically drained. I cannot imagine what it might be like, when you are unable to share the care of your child who has so many additional needs, and quite honestly, I am in awe of you.

The *good news* is that during this time one thing that has really stuck out for me is how the work of carers is being recognised and validated. You will just have to trust me when I say that there are people who will continue to fight and raise awareness in all areas. We want to shout from the rooftops that our carers and parent carers need support too.

We all know about all of the issues I have touched on, but imagine how terrifying this must be for an anxious child. With social media bringing the world closer, it must appear that all of this is happening just a stone's throw away from the safe confines of their bedroom walls.

We should therefore not be that surprised that sometimes they do not want to get out of their beds. Also, to avoid disappointment, they do not allow themselves to have the dreams and aspirations for the future that we did at their age.

I sleep a little easier at night as my faith in a merciful God lets me dare believe he will intervene and raise some powerful people up to stand up for our beautiful planet before it is too late. However, that is little comfort to any who do not have the same beliefs, and I understand it is a hard stretch for many.

We naturally like things to be backed up by scientific proof, and I know from having conversations with my son that he needs tangible answers to the many questions he has.

It is so easy to stick our heads in the sand because all these issues appear completely insurmountable. I guess in some respects a lot of us have lived a substantial proportion of our lives, but our children have only just started theirs, so it would make sense that these issues are more of a big deal to them.

There is a message of hope that is weaved through these pages, but as a parent who has stayed up in the wee hours trying to soothe an anxious child, I am at a little bit of a loss as to how I can offer comfort when it comes to these huge issues.

If you are like me, then I appreciate how you may struggle with not finding a solution or having the ability or superpowers to make it better. The sad fact is that in a particular moment of drama with a child, there is little we can do with regards to climate change or the rain forest inferno or answering questions on the aftermath of Covid-19.

But what we can do is this. We can take our children's worries seriously and respond with compassion, even though we may not fully understand the situation or their associated fears.

For example, if you ask your child what is on their minds and they respond with something huge, that is out of your control, you could say something like, *I am so sorry; it is an awful situation, and I can understand why you must be so upset.*

This response shows that even though you may not understand the ins and outs of what they are worrying about, what you do acknowledge and understand is the fact they are worried.

I learnt that even when my child was frustrated when they felt depressed and did not know why the most important thing I could do was recognise their feelings. The whys or wherefores were pretty much irrelevant.

You remember what we said about needing compassion more than understanding. Well, you can see how perhaps we apply that, albeit subconsciously, to our children too.

As a parent, it is comforting to be able to offer support in that way, as often there are no obvious quick fixes, and if you are anything like me that is what your brain defaults to.

We can also ask questions because it is my experience that our young people may know a lot more than we give them credit for. Asking questions and listening to the answers are a way of showing our children that we do care. We are taking the time to listen to them to try and understand their anxieties, and this will also help you build trust that they can talk to you about anything.

Perhaps if you ask your child what the matter is and the answer they give completely floors you, you could say:-

I would be really interested in learning more about that as it's not something I know much about.

Or

That sounds awful. It must be really hard to get your head around. I'm struggling too, so how do you cope with that?

Do you remember a time when you were a kid, and you were able to share with an adult new information, and how important that made you feel? Well, I believe it is no different for our children. By acknowledging and asking questions, we are inflating their important bubble, and boosting their confidence. Like me, you may learn some really interesting stuff along the way.

I hope this gives you a little insight into what might be bugging your kids because being able to do even the tiniest thing to help your child feel better brings some peace.

Later, we will look at some ways you can offer some accessible practical self-care for them.

In the meantime, and back to the world-sized problems. I will be supporting my son when he strikes for climate change and I will continue to champion the amazing young people like Greta Thunberg who are taking a stand. I will encourage conversation about these difficult subjects and make more of an effort to try and keep informed and expand my knowledge, even though it makes for some exceedingly difficult reading. I will do my absolute best to try and understand because it is my belief that this is what they need. The fact that they know you are taking their concerns seriously brings our children a special type of comfort.

What will you try and help your children with? Maybe, you can think of some things that you could engage your child in conversation with. Perhaps they have certain interests, or there may be things they have expressed an opinion on in the past.

It may also be worth taking some time and thinking about how you may respond to some of the bigger questions that may crop up too.

It is a great way of building trust, and one of the benefits is that it may help pave the way to giving them confidence in sharing some personal stuff too. We will look at that in more detail in Chapter 13.

We have explored some of the issues that worry our children and recognised how their mental health can be affected by some of the huge expectations that society places on them. But what about those expectations that are closer to home?

In the next chapter, we will have a look at how it is possible to manage these expectations and how that can be beneficial for the whole family.

CHAPTER 12

Managing Expectations

IN THE LAST CHAPTER, we looked at some of the things that worry our children and cause them sleepless nights. What is more valuable than knowledge to us as parents is having some practical things we can do. Even the small things can contribute to making their lives a little easier.

Understanding and knowing when to apply them not only makes for a happier child, but it may also enable you to have some more space to concentrate on your own self-care. Shortly we will have a look at some of the practical ways we can help our child.

First, let's talk about managing expectations. I'd like to have a few words on the subject of spoons - an idea that was incredibly beneficial to the whole family once I'd wrapped my head around the idea.

You may get to this point and think, she has finally lost it, but bear with me, because this is interesting, completely doable, free and may just be a game-changer.

What do I mean by managing expectations?

My teenager came to me one day and asked, "do you know about the Spoon Theory?" I wracked my brain, as I imagine you are doing if you do not already know, wondering what it is all about. Now, and although I revel in the smugness of knowing about some of this teenagerly type stuff, I had to admit defeat on this one. However, once I understood the concept it quickly became part of our household's daily conversations. I believe it could be a useful tool for you, and anything that helps and is free has got to be a no-brainer.

Here is what I found out: -

'Originally created by Christine Miserandino in 2003 as she tried to come up with a way to explain how lupus (an autoimmune condition) makes her feel to a long-time friend at dinner, she tried using spoons from tables around them as props. She discovered that they were a quirky, easy to understand way of explaining the little things that can actually be huge hurdles for those who struggle with their energy levels'. -Bonnie Evie Gifford, Happiful Magazine.

The idea is that we use quantities of *spoons* to describe our energy levels at one given point. We all start the day with a different number of spoons, based on such criteria as physical or mental illness, whether we are sleeping well and have a good diet, what our week has been like so far, etc.

To explain this more clearly below is a scenario for two vastly different people, and bear in mind there is a cost for every task, action, or interaction.

Mr X

Mr X is reasonably healthy and does not suffer from any mental or physical illness. He has had a good week so far, so he is fortunate to start his new day with 100 spoons.

He gets up after a refreshing night's sleep feeling positive about the day ahead, makes himself some breakfast and a cup of coffee, kisses his wife and kids then sets out in his nicely air-conditioned comfortable car and arrives at his office building in plenty of time. The cost to Mr X thanks to this great start is just 5 spoons and he has plenty to last him for the rest of the day, or so he thinks. However, and such is life, things do not continue so well for Mr X.

He has a difficult meeting that day and leaves work feeling stressed and frustrated. He gets home to deal with the fallout after his wife has had a hard day with whingy kids. He has no spoons left. Then he goes to bed. He tosses and turns all night thinking about the terrible meeting he had and wakes after a dreadful night's sleep. His spoon count for the beginning of the next day has dwindled to a measly 60. He forces himself out of bed, finds there is no milk for his coffee, and is late for work after sitting in traffic.

This disastrous start to the day has cost him half of his remaining spoon allowance. Now he only has thirty spoons left, and there's a lot of things to do today. Therefore, he needs to be careful because what he is left with has suddenly become a lot more precious.

Below is a different scenario of a young person who struggles with their mental health. Let's say for argument's sake, they suffer from extreme anxiety.

Mr Y

Mr Y has already had a harrowing week as his anxiety levels have been off the charts. There has been nothing in particular that has caused this, it's just how his body reacts to everyday life. He wakes that morning after a restless night with 50 spoons.

He talks himself into getting out of bed and getting dressed. Even brushing his teeth is a supreme effort. He does not eat breakfast as he is too churned up about the thought of the day ahead to eat anything and eventually leaves the house. This has already cost him 20 spoons.

He travels on public transport, which is loud and busy. A stranger brushes up against him which he does not like and this cost him 15 spoons. He reaches his destination and now faces the whole day ahead with just 5 remaining spoons. When he gets home, someone asks him how his day went and what he wants for tea. He does not have enough spoons left even to make a simple choice.

We can see from this how different situations and scenarios can seriously alter how we feel and act. This idea really helped me appreciate how a normal day can affect our energy levels. Once you add to that the struggle that mental illness causes, we can perhaps start to see how intolerable simple life can be.

I used the following illustration once to try and explain this.

Imagine running up and downstairs 10 times without stopping – even a reasonably fit person would be a little out of breath after that. Now imagine doing exactly the same thing but with a broken leg. It sounds a bit brutal but at the same time if you ever need to get this particular point across it's quite effective.

Why try the Spoon Theory?

When I was diagnosed with ME, which I believe was a result of the stress levels my body had been under, one of the best pieces of advice I was given was to imagine my energy levels as currency.

Some days would cost me more than others and some things were worth saving for. Sometimes I was going to go overdrawn, and on occasions that was worth the cost. On other occasions, it was a learning experience that taught me how to pace myself.

This has been extraordinarily useful to me. I am aware however that talking about money can be anxiety-provoking. It seems to me therefore that using the metaphor of spoons is a much more accessible and friendly way of getting our heads around this.

Another thing that has become apparent, after utilising this tool, is that energy levels go up and down according to levels of anxiety. For example, a typical school day would have cost my son 100 spoons and the effort of just attending and recovery time needed after a bad day led to many sick days. However, put him at a huge concert at Birmingham

O2 Arena, in the center of the mosh pit, surrounded by people he did not know on every side, packed in very tightly may only have cost him 50 spoons.

The reason for this is very telling and quite simple. At that moment he was not in a toxic environment where a cruel word from classmates would cripple him, but instead, here amid these jostling strangers, he was not judged or picked on or bullied! He was with me, doing one of his favourite things in the world and that meant so much to him. His anxiety had literally been drowned out by the wonderful atmosphere and brilliant music, and he knew that everyone around him could not have cared about anything he was doing as they were consumed by the same thing.

So, I hope that has helped explain the Spoon Theory. I am sure you can see the benefits of understanding how different lifestyle scenarios, issues and, health problems can affect the number of spoons we have to play with. We can also see how our spoons are indeed a precious currency.

How about taking this a step further and apply this practically by considering creating a chart with your child?

Your Spoon Chart

This could be a great way of letting your child know you understand how everyday life affects their mood and energy levels. Perhaps you could explain the theory to them (if they don't already know) and even have some fun discussing how many spoons they think certain activities cost them.

You could set up a simple chart. For example, just use three columns and the headings *activity*, *spoon cost,* and *spoon balance.* At the top put the number of spoons your child thinks they start the day with. Then list all of the things that are part of everyday life, the cost for each one, and the balance left after each activity. Pretty much like you would set up a very simple budget. It's just energy instead of money.

To get you started, here are some ideas of activities you could include, and some things to consider when you are allocating your spoons.

Getting out of bed

As we have discussed this can be an immense effort for those who are struggling with anxiety, and it is a good opportunity to let your child know that you recognise this.

Getting dressed

Deciding what to wear can be exhausting. For a child with anxiety making any sort of decision will cost them dearly. Again, reassure them you get this.

Leaving the house

This is a biggie. Perhaps look at deciding which trips are worth the spoons they cost. For example, they may consider that going to McDonald's is worth the spoons and accompanying you to do the weekly shop is not (who knew).

Spending time with family and friends

I do not know how you feel, but I find even spending a happy relaxed time with my nearest and dearest can be draining. If your child is anxious, they may feel they have to put a face on around other people, and as we have discussed keeping up appearances can be utterly exhausting.

It is also important to bear in mind that some things are worth saving for. If you know there is something coming up, like a family get together, a trip to the cinema or a sleepover at a friend's, you may find it beneficial to suggest that your child gets plenty of rest beforehand. You could tell them that they are effectively saving their spoons.

You could give them the incentive that, if they are well-rested, they are likely to enjoy what they are doing a lot more. It will also help them to understand that they can't go 100 miles per hour, they need to sleep, stop, and consider what is important to them. This will add positive enforcement and help your child feel like they have strategies to cope with these situations.

Perhaps you could look at some different scenarios with your child, and don't forget your self-care too. Where are your spoons getting used up?

I have learnt over the years that some things are just worth going overdrawn for, and to illustrate that I just want to tie this section off neatly with a little bow by sharing this memory with you.

I will never forget the moment at that Panic At The Disco concert in the O2, standing in that mosh pit with my son, his friends and, a whole lot of strangers. Brendan Urie (lead singer and not at all unpleasant to look at – seriously you should Google him) was playing the piano suspended above the crowd.

It was one of our favourite songs and when I looked over at my son tears were streaming down his face. He was singing his heart out! It was one of the happiest, proudest moments of my life. Here was my boy who had so much courage and had fought his anxiety to be here. For this moment he was living his life, doing what other *normal* teenagers were doing, and loving every minute of it regardless of how many spoons it had cost him.

See? Some things are worth saving up for.

I hope as you read this that it has bought to mind some memories you have and that you will have peace of mind that sometimes having to make time for a recovery period after an amazing experience like that is something you would consider is worth paying for sometimes.

You may find that using the language of spoons is a really useful tool, as you have demonstrated to your child that you understand that sometimes things are a huge effort for them, and you have opened up an ongoing conversation.

That, in itself, is valuable because I understand how difficult it is sometimes to talk to our children. Most importantly you have provided some information that is pure gold when you are teaching your child how to manage their health.

Remember how we touched on the subject of talking to your child about their mental health, and how you may broach that subject. This may be a really good way in. From experience, I have found that it has been a really helpful tool when I have been speaking to my children, and I hope it will be good for you too.

In the next chapter, I want to go into more detail about how we may open the conversation, and how this can be incredibly helpful and healing to both you and your child.

CHAPTER 13

Talking Mental Health

In the last chapter, we looked at how recognising the effort and energy it took to do everyday things was just another thing to help you build trust and understanding with regards to their mental health. In this chapter, we are going to take that a step further by exploring how we can engage our children in talking about how they feel.

I have sat with a lot of parent carers in the past who have had older children, and they have expressed a profound desire to be able to understand their child better. I imagine you have yearned for the same and I see you.

Perhaps you have been in a situation when you have wanted to start a conversation, but it felt like there were too many obstacles in your way. These sentiments may strike a chord with you:

If only I could ask them how they feel without them getting angry or upset.

Or

If I just knew what might help, I could make their day a bit better.

Or

I really want to help, but I dare not bring up the subject because it might remind them of how awful they feel.

Then there are times where you have a good day or few days, they seem better and it seems an ideal opportunity to chat about things, but you just don't want to rock the boat.

Yep – I thought so.

Very often, because a question can appear so loaded, we may not be able to see how to tackle it, and the more we let it stew in our brain the bigger the barrier to conversation becomes. Someone once described this to me as a starfish turning into a Kracken (terrifying mythological sea creature).

But asking the question *what can I do to help* is important. As we have discussed with the world issues, if we know even the littlest things that may improve the situation for our child, I am sure you will agree that the answer is pure gold.

I don't know much about battling large scary ocean dwellers, but I have had a bit of experience talking to my two boys.

The first thing I want to share with you is in relation to opening the conversation with your child.

It is especially important; in fact, I would say crucial, that when you ask *what can I do to help,* ask them when they are in a good place.

If you pose that question when, for argument's sake, they are in the middle of a meltdown, you are not going to get the desired answer. They are not in a place where they can express themselves and are highly likely to be out of spoons. Being asked a question like that, which needs some serious directed thought, will just add to their anxieties. It is also likely that it will not be processed properly, and you may well get the blame for not knowing what to do in the first place!

If, however, you can find a moment when things are peaceful when you are perhaps relaxing together and they are in a good place, they can ponder it stress-free before they present you with an answer.

Remember – no one knows your child as well as you do, and you will know some things that help already, but I believe you can never have too much information. The more you know, the more prepared you can be.

It is really healthy for your child to be able to express what they need, and if you think that your child may be overwhelmed trying to come up with an answer or it is age-appropriate, you could always brainstorm with them. Why not make it into a fun activity. Grab a bit piece of paper and coloured pens and write, doodle, draw and scribble.

As I said before, you might be able to nudge them towards things you feel are good for them, and this will help their confidence in coming up with more ideas.

Get the conversation started

That conversation can give you some valuable information that will give you peace of mind that, when they need it, you can make a positive difference. Also, you have yet again demonstrated understanding, which means when the time comes for you to intervene, you will already have reduced their anxiety.

My son has expressed the sentiment that I know what he needs goes a long way to reduce his anxiety.

Use Simple Language

Another thing that may help if you are trying to encourage conversation with your child is to once again opt for simple language. You could say something like: -

You know those times when you are struggling, I just wondered is there anything I can do which might help a bit. Perhaps have a think and let me know?

The same simple language you can be used to speak to your GP about how you feel can be used when you are chatting with your child. As we have learnt, simple language will help your child explain how they are feeling. You will appreciate that explaining to someone how you feel can be draining and expressing it might feel like affirming it.

If you have struggled with this, imagine how much harder it must be for your child. For example, let's take a common ailment like a headache again, which for most is a mild irritation. If someone asks, *how are you,* what would you say?

Yep, absolutely we would simply say: - *I have a headache.* We wouldn't say my muscles and blood vessels have swollen and tightened and are now putting pressure on my surrounding nerves causing a rush of pain right into my brain.

That sounds utterly terrifying, and you may feel more inclined to call an ambulance than simply to take a couple of paracetamols.

In my experience, there is no difference when you are trying to explain to someone what depression or anxiety feels like. If you are already feeling awful the last thing you need is to hear yourself say something like: -

I feel horrible, it's like the whole world is crashing in and I am convinced something horrible is going to happen. On top of that, I feel like there is this huge dark chasm in my stomach and my heart is beating so fast it feels like it is going to explode from my chest.

I do not know about you but by now I would feel even worse and possibly quite frightened.

The Power of Words

So, instead of that long and detailed description of our feelings, we have a word in our house that sums all of that up, and it is simply *struggling.*

It is brilliant and really works on many different levels. It immediately eliminates the need for any explanation, reduces the distress and confusion and everyone intuitively knows what is needed because we've already had the *what can I do to help* conversations.

Perhaps, now you have this new knowledge, you could talk in the language of spoons.

As my son explained to me, sometimes when like Mr Y he got home and had nothing left to give, he could just say, *Mum, I'm really struggling.*

Perhaps when your child has been able to tell you what it is that helps them feel better, you could also suggest that you come up with a word that bypasses all those difficult feelings. A word that lets you and those around them know that they are *struggling.*

These are just a few things that I have learnt which have not only been useful but have been a wonderful way of reducing anxiety for us all. Even if your children are smaller, you could perhaps come up with some fun words to express how they are feeling, so that when they are in the middle of one of those, *I am past it and I don't know what to do with myself tantrums* you could just use it so they know you know. For example, I'm feeling *funny.* It's *difficult,* My *head is busy.*

I am sure you will come up with lots of your own strategies of how to best talk to your children, but if you have struggled in the past, I hope this has been of some help to you.

Now we have looked at the practical application and reaped the rewards of managing expectations, and hopefully got our kids talking, we can now look at some practical things we can do to comfort and soothe our children.

CHAPTER 14

Practical Tips for your Child's Well-Being

EARLY ON WE HAD a look at some of the ideas that can boost our well-being as a parent carer. In this chapter, we will now look at some of the things I have found that have helped my children when they have needed some extra *tender loving care.*

Gruntling

If you look in the dictionary, you will find the definition of *gruntling* as a young pig or hog, but you will not find our definition for it.

Over the years and since our boys were little, we have invented several words in our family. Much like you might invent a nickname or change the name of something because that is how your child first pronounced it and it was unbelievably cute.

For example, a cucumber is a *cumberbumber* an elbow is your *armbow* (well doesn't that make perfect sense), and perhaps one of my favourites - the common rhino will forever be known in our house as a *rhinososososos*.

The origin of our definition of *gruntling* is remarkably simple – to be *gruntled* is quite simply the opposite of being disgruntled, which according to the Cambridge English Dictionary is being *unhappy, annoyed, and disappointed by something.* So *gruntling* is the practice of making someone happy and calm and doing your best to take away disappointment.

We all think it's kinda cool, and your own version of *gruntling* can be a really useful and effective tool when helping your child.

I am sure you have a first aid kit for physical injuries somewhere accessible. After all plasters and Germolene are part and parcel of everyday life and children are always getting bumped and grazed. As we know their injuries are not always physical, so just as we have created one for you, let's build up a first aid kit for your child's mental well-being that you can have on hand too.

We all have things that bring us comfort and help when we are *struggling*! In my experience when it comes to young people, and especially those with sensory issues, that this is, even more, the case. Being able to identify those items or actions which can *gruntle* our child can be an enormous help and comfort when they are struggling with their mental health.

Gruntling for my youngest looks like this. A drinkable cup of tea in a particular mug made by me with a straw (the sensation of the hot liquid is very soothing), pasta and cheese with lots of black pepper, and a hot water bottle. He may also like to sit down and watch a favourite show or film. He has discovered these things over time, but now when he says he is *struggling* the first aid kit comes out and the *gruntling* commences.

It does not have to be complicated, but it can be extremely effective especially when administered straight away.

I have found that some of the most effective tools are those that we remember using when our children are little. It has been proven that when under stress or struggling with mood, children may self - soothe by regressing a little. Therefore, it makes a lot of sense that some of the sensory things that perhaps worked for them when they were young, may also work now.

I know that every child is different, and for some having their childhood cuddly toy is a huge comfort, where for others they would be mortified even knowing someone knew they had still held onto it.

You know your child best and know what they need, but as we have discussed if you can ask them what makes them feel better, it will give you some ideas of practical things you can put together.

Why not get out the paper and pens again and have a brainstorm.

To get you started let's refer once more to our comfort box. This has been something that has been incredibly effective with my son, and it is something that can be used time and time again.

Comfort Boxes

Remember we spoke about the comfort box you could have that had accessible things to help you relax when you had those precious free moments? Well, why not create one for your child too?

You could buy, make, find and/or decorate the box together, and choose the things that go inside. This is a box that they can go to if they are feeling anxious or depressed, and there will be something in there that can help. To get you started, here are some ideas of the things my son has had in his box over the years.

- Paper and pens.
- Colouring book (we found some that were age-appropriate, featuring his favourite characters or TV of film and that was even better).
- Slime (what child/teenager doesn't love this) – there are all sorts of different types and textures and it can be an excellent sensory activity.
- Stress ball.
- Magazine with activities.
- Fiddle toys.
- Sachet of hot chocolate.
- Bath bombs (having a good soak can work wonders).
- A little craft activity (you can buy these reasonably cheaply, and because they contain all the materials you need in one

place there is no scrabbling about trying to find the things you need).

- One of his favourite cuddlies or toys. Obviously, not the one that is surgically attached to him at the time but re-discovering another favourite treasure inside can be effective.

You can also swap things out and switch things up or come up with little surprises that you can drop in there for them to discover – like a Freddo, or a new book from a series they like, or a note telling them how much they are loved. Also bear in mind that the box does not just have to contain all new things, some of the most comforting are the most familiar.

Really it is anything that will help soothe your child as soon as the lid comes off, and if you think of things that they can do on their own, well that gives you a little bit of time to yourself.

For my son, knowing a box like this existed did a lot to lower his anxiety in itself, and he knew that he could find something inside that would offer a welcome distraction when he was having a particularly hard time.

You may also remember when we were discussing what to put into your comfort box, I very briefly mentioned the idea of journaling, and I just wanted to go into a little more detail here.

Journaling

If you have started your own journal, you could show your child (our own enthusiasm for something can be quite contagious). If not perhaps start one with them. You could start with writing some things down that make them happy (a version of things to be grateful for) or even get them to express this by drawing pictures. A good place to start is by writing some headings on the top of the pages.

How about:-

If I could try something new it would be...

Or

If I could have any pet it would be ...

Or

Things I would like to do with my friends are...

This is a great way to get them thinking about positive things, and if they have had trouble thinking about the future, this may be a less scary way to introduce that.

Also, one of the most difficult things my son had to face was when he had started working with a therapist was filling in a form on a twice-daily basis with regards to his feelings. Remember what I said about avoiding emotive words when talking to our children about their health? The way the forms were set out meant that they had failed on that point miserably. No child wants to look at a form that asks such questions as:-

Have you had any thoughts about harming yourself today?

My son found a much better way of recording this information in his journal, and this may prove quite useful if you are in that situation. He got a piece of graph paper, and every day he filled in each square with the appropriate colour, according to the colour key he had produced. For instance, feeling good was yellow, so he would colour in the square yellow. Feeling tired was green, so he would fill in the square in the colour green. Blue was unhappy etc. Sometimes he split the square into two if he felt his mood had been a bit up and down that day.

The beauty of this was that he could add to his colour key when he felt like it or it was appropriate so that the ways of describing his feelings were not limited. He may even have had a colour for feeling unhappy today but better than yesterday!

It avoided having to look at depressing forms and his therapist was still able to gauge his feelings, and also see any patterns that had emerged more clearly than if she had had to collate lots of paperwork.

There was a huge benefit to being able to express his feeling in the way he had chosen for himself. In those moments, like Mr Y when he had exhausted his spoons, it was another way he could communicate his feeling to us.

Other Useful *Gruntling* Tools

Some other things that have helped us were music/audiobooks and playlists. My son has put together a playlist of songs that are particularly comforting or uplifting. When I hear these selections of songs, I know he is delicate without him having to go through the stress of explaining it to me.

When he was younger, he used to go to sleep listening to Stephen Fry reading Harry Potter. (on CD, not in person, although I'm sure he would have loved that). He has told me since how comforting that was. It was something familiar and he was able to shut his anxious head off for a while. Being immersed in the magical world of Hogwarts allowed him to drift off into a peaceful sleep.

Also, for younger children, in particular, a recording of our voice reading their favourite stories can be effective as well. It serves as a comfort to them and helps preserve a bit of our very precious feeling of calm.

A tip for bedtime for the younger ones too – give them an item of your clothing with your familiar smell on it. In the past I have either taken off a top I have been wearing that day or sprayed something lightly with my perfume and then left it ready to give them at bedtime. We sometimes forget about the other senses other than sight and hearing and a familiar smell, the same smell they get when you cuddle them can be amazingly effective.

I hope you can see how valuable it is to be able to ask your child what it is that makes them feel better, but just as valuable is your instinct as a parent. You know your child best and therefore understand how they tick and what they need when it all gets a bit too much.

Having something practical to use has been incredibly useful to me over the years, and I am sure having some things on hand will afford you a little more peace as well.

Before I wrap up this chapter, there are just two other things that I have come to realise that may help in making the soothing process go that little more smoothly.

Watch the Signs

In my experience, when you are dealing with a child who struggles with an illness where one of the symptoms is heightened senses, there will be times when your child just does not want to be touched. I am sure you will identify with the feeling when all of your parenting muscles are just straining to wrap them in your arms, and yet doing that just adds fuel to the fire.

If it is some comfort, my son has assured me that during these times he has recognised and appreciates that it has been difficult for me not to respond physically. But the fact that I respect his needs and wishes at that point has itself been comforting for him.

I have now learnt not to assume to know what he wants just because it makes sense to me but to listen and familiarise myself with the signs and the circumstances, and when possible be led by him.

We Choose Our Battles - Know What's Best

Something else which is worth bearing in mind is that very often your child may not know that they need some *first aid*.

I am sure we all remember those toddler tantrums where our children would just be beside themselves, very often because they were exhausted and overtired. Our older children can often display their own versions of those tantrums, but the catalyst is the same. Living with any form of illness is exhausting and very often they just get past it. Even when he says he does not want it, presenting my son with his cup of tea and cheesy pasta can go a long way and help speed up his recovery.

Therefore, sometimes when your child is adamant that going and spending time with his friends is what is going to make him feel better, he may need something completely different.

I have learnt that I do not always get it right, and more importantly, have also learnt not to beat myself up about it. Children, especially teenagers, are a very strange, contrary, and often cryptic breed. We are not suddenly blessed with mind-reading capabilities when we become a parent, so it is difficult to know for sure. We can only take a deep breath, remind ourselves we are doing OK, and reach for an alternative from the comfort box or first aid kit.

On those occasions, we do get it right, tick the box, bank the win, and be content on that occasion. We have been able to give them not necessarily what they want, but more importantly what they really need.

I hope you have found the information in this section helpful and that you have lots of ideas to help build up your child's well-being first aid kit and have discovered some practical things you could try. I hope it brings you some relief that there are things you can do to improve things.

To tie off this section I would like to offer you some extra comfort. I have been told by both my children, that even just being there for them and understanding some of their needs makes a huge difference to them at the time. Do you see it can be as simple as that?

So now we know a little more about self-care for us, and we have some ways we can help our children, I want to share with you the next part of the journey.

In the next section, I want to show you there is life outside the storm, a life full of new opportunities and possibilities. Even though you will be battered and battle-weary, if you continue to take care of yourself and be gentle to your fragile self you will be able to walk that road to recovery with new confidence.

SECTION 3

To Recovery and Beyond

REMEMBER WHEN I described the lull when the adrenalin subsides, the earthquake has quietened, and all the nasties have crawled back into their dark hole. Well, that's when I found I could stop and take a deep breath.

It is my hope that sharing a bit of the journey that got me to where I am now will inspire you to keep moving forward, motivate you to keep up with the self-care and have the confidence to breathe a little more freely and deeply.

I would like to help you find your feet again after the trauma you have been through, to learn, to be at peace with how this experience may have changed you, and how I found and still find that recovery is an ongoing process.

CHAPTER 15

Out of the Storm
- What now?

THERE CAME A TIME not so long ago when things started to improve. My children were more settled, and therefore so was I. Their recovery took them off in different directions, all of a sudden that peace that in the past was elusive stayed for a while, and I found myself in another weird space.

I can remember always thinking I would dread the moment when my offspring had flown the nest, and I had spoken to folk with older children who had described this as just a new stage in life. However, after being so involved in their care sometimes to the point where that very thing took all my time and energy, not having that familiar intensity in my life left a gaping hole. I can remember thinking, *what do I do with this? What now?*

I am sure you have been in that position when you have wished for change, especially in the early days with your child's development or even health. I can remember looking at my baby laying on his back playing with the jungle gym and thinking I cannot wait until you are more mobile. Then when that day came, I was run ragged following him around.

I was constantly on high alert making sure he did not put his chubby fingers into anything he shouldn't and checking the stair gate for the hundredth time that day (which is ridiculous because those things are impossible for adults never mind toddlers). I found myself thinking that I wished he was a little less mobile. I am sure that you are nodding your head at that one as you remember those familiar feelings.

In the same way, I can remember understandably thinking that I can't wait until my children get to the stage when they feel well and able to be more independent, and I can have a little more time to be myself.

In the early days, I can remember thinking now when they are OK, I will be OK too. I really had no clue about what to do with all of this *me-time* once I had it.

The big lesson I learnt during that time was this. Even though life is vastly different now, and there are so many more positives, the biggest being improved physical and mental health all round, some days those difficult moments and memories from the past just come back and bite you.

Quite often these feelings come out of the blue, and when they do, quite frankly, it can feel like you have been hit by a train.

Remember I talked about trauma being like an open wound? Well, just as you must give physical injuries time to heal you have to be realistic about that healing time, I have found it is the same for psychological injury.

Although I have had a professional look at my wounds, I have had them cleaned and the course of anti-biotics (actually more than one course) and they look fine on the surface, some days that scar burns and itches.

What can we do when that happens? Perhaps, the first thing is to recognise we may be in denial about being *fine*, recognise that in fact, we are not *fine*, and accept that fact.

In those early days, when I had found my way out of the storm, and woke feeling awful, my default was to think all those negative things about myself once again. They would go something like this:-

I shouldn't feel like this.

I'm stupid for feeling like this, I should be able to cope now.

I cannot figure out what is wrong with me, therefore there cannot be anything wrong with me, I need to pull myself together.

I should have moved on by now.

You may have been in that place where you have felt those sentiments, especially when there is nothing you can put your finger on that should make you feel like that. I have learnt that during those times there is often actually a lot going on internally, externally, or both. Someone once explained this to me in a way that I found very helpful, and which I will try now to share with you. It helped immensely to know a little of what is going on in my brain during these times, and I hope it may take a little of the fear out of it for you too. It will hopefully give you a little insight into why we get these bolts out of the blue, these sudden, unpleasant, disruptive thoughts that knock us off our feet.

They explained this process to me.

A man who had struggled with severe anxiety most of his life, and who would literally fall to pieces when he heard raised voices, was finally, with the help of a therapist, able to attribute this behaviour to a childhood memory.

As a child, the end of the day was his favourite time. This was the time that his father returned home from work. Every day, for as long as he remembered, he would run to meet his father and his father would respond by picking him up, giving him a hug, and asking him about his day.

One evening his father was late. When he did get home after a really hard day and his son ran to meet him, his father shouted at him to leave him alone.

For this little boy, that was a traumatic experience. The sudden and unexpected raised angry voice of his father sent his body into fight or flight, and in that moment his little brain could not process just what was going on.

Most of our memories are stored in the part of the brain where they are able to be processed correctly. These memories can be activated or accessed at any point. You know that feeling when you hear a particular song or just get a hint of perfume and it takes you back to a setting or scenario, that is how memories should work.

Our traumatic memories do not fare so well. Our brain has not been able to process them in the same way, so they go to the same part of the brain that deals with fight or flight. Can you imagine the standoff with the saber-toothed tiger where a prehistoric man would run away or attack the threat? Because of this storage problem, when that traumatic memory is accessed it comes back with all the original sights, smells, and feelings associated with the original trauma. In short, it can feel like being hit by a wrecking ball.

So, let's go back to the story of the man struggling with anxiety and have a look at the outcome - there is a happy ending.

After years of struggling with PTSD (Post Traumatic Stress Disorder), he was able to access that difficult memory, in a safe and controlled setting. His therapist was able to explain that how as a little boy, that isolated incident of being yelled at by someone who never raised their voice before, had such a profound effect on him for all those years.

In quite simple terms the wayward memory, through that therapy session, was popped back into the correct storage, and when it was recalled it did not come back with all the bells and whistles and negative feelings, it came back as just what it was – a memory.

It is incredible how certain triggers can cause such disruptive reactions, but having an explanation, even a very simple one, can help deal with the fear of the unknown. A little knowledge can go a long way to aiding recovery.

I hope you found that interesting. But more important than having an explanation as to why we are feeling the way we are, is to acknowledge our feelings, and to, once again, look towards self-care.

Sometimes it is possible to plan for these things too, as very often we may recognise a pattern, or there may be certain days that we find particularly difficult. For example, here is an example of something I have learnt to deal with.

Every year, a week or so before my birthday, I start feeling very negative and I struggle. A big black cloud descends, and I feel absolutely awful. I cannot really pinpoint exactly why, there have definitely been difficult times around that time, maybe more than a few. But if you asked, I would not be able to tell you exactly what was up.

In the past, when I got tearful, short-tempered, angry, depressed, anxious, irrational, or if my wonderful long-suffering family were especially unlucky all the above, I could not figure out why. I found that frustrating, and you guessed it, it was straight back to the default of *I should not be feeling like this!*

Everything was fine, the kids were not struggling, nothing had broken, exploded, or imploded, so *I don't know why I felt like this.*

It would not surprise me if you have had many moments like this, especially later on in your journey, when perhaps a lot of your energy reserves have been used up. When you are recovering from a difficult time, and because in the past you have been so consumed with the care of your child, once again to acknowledge feelings like this can feel a little alien.

You and I now know better. It's amazing how hard and downright cruel we can be to ourselves when there is no obvious trigger for our negative feelings. We frighten ourselves with our negative thoughts and beat ourselves up with unkind words. Although I have learnt to recognise these thoughts, it still does not mean I am a constant ray of sunshine. To be honest, I don't know anyone who is, but it does mean I am deliberate about being kinder to myself as I hope you will be too.

Another thing is that I have found very helpful is being aware of those patterns, those days you may find particularly difficult and have a plan of action. We can have a look at that a bit later on.

Dates that Come Back to Bite Us

I am fairly sure that there will be dates stamped on your brain, other than those celebratory anniversaries. We are all wired differently and for some those dates are ones that can be recalled in a heartbeat.

Whether they are ones that make you smile or others that make you feel sick to your stomach, remember you have the confidence to be more honest about your feelings now, and hopefully you have learnt to be a little kinder to yourself.

You know that taking care of yourself is completely appropriate and healthy. It may be one of those times where spending some time chatting over a coffee or having a good heart to heart with someone who is in your support network is just what the doctor ordered.

With regards to those fleeting thoughts, in therapy I was told to acknowledge them, validate them, and give myself permission to respond to them however I needed to. For example, when those blues come knocking, I now think to myself:

Right, I am feeling a bit low, but that's OK and I am not going to beat myself about it.

Now that I have had a little practice my next thought is:

What can I do about it?

I reach for something in my own self-care first aid kit.

We all have difficult memories and as I have already mentioned, some of them are so strong and stubbornly embedded that we not only associate dates and places with these, but we may also even remember smells and sounds associated with them. Something I have picked up, which can be helpful on these days, is learning how to reclaim them. It is possible to take something that was a hard memory and make a new memory that you can attach to it.

Please remember these are just things that have worked for me, and it is something I have done slowly and carefully. You may still be very fragile as I was, so it is important not to push yourself and do only what you are comfortable with. It takes practice.

But to give you an idea - this year when the birthday blues began to descend my wonderfully wise son suggested we did some fun things leading up to the day to distract me. This really helped and slowly I am learning how to reclaim my memories, so I can look forward to my birthday instead of dreading the run-up to it.

I have the comfort that those around me know I *struggle* around that time and don't judge me. I have also learnt to listen to the voices of those around me, my support network who know me, love, and care about me and will be honest, instead of the negative ones that echo in my head.

So, on those difficult days, once I have had a little bit of a strop (as I have said it's a process), I consciously think about the kind words others have spoken, and I drag my thought process kicking and screaming to the following conclusion:

I am giving myself complete permission to feel like this. I do not know why, but that does not matter. What matters is that I am feeling lousy and I need to take care of myself and be as kind to myself as I would to someone else who was feeling the same way.

What can you say to yourself? Who do you need to listen to, so you can soak up some kind words of encouragement? What are the memories that you could start creating happier vibes around?

It definitely takes time and a little practice to start thinking like this but don't give up, because now you have the incentive of knowing that taking care of your well-being is not only beneficial to you but also to those around you.

You have some great new coping strategies you are working on so you will be OK, and it will keep getting better.

Now we have looked a little about moving from out of the storm into an unknown world let's explore how you recover when the rest of the world is trying to dictate that very recovery for you.

CHAPTER 16

Recovery in Your Time

WHEN WE SPOKE ABOUT your support network, we looked at the fact that some of the people who come into your life may not be helpful to your recovery. It is my experience that there are also people that you are likely to come across those who very kindly wish to tell you how and when you should recover. I include this because I would hate you to fall victim to this so far into your journey.

These are people who think they know exactly how you feel and will try and jolly you into feeling better. They may make you feel like you should be over this already and need to move on. They are likely to have never experienced what it is like to care for a poorly child, and mental health may be something that is completely alien to them.

I am pretty convinced that when people make these helpful comments, they are only doing it from the goodness of their heart, but please don't ever be pushed into pretending to feel better. There is no shame in how you are feeling, and people's healing time differs a lot.

You are entering a new stage in your life where hopefully things are changing for the better for you and your child, and as such, you may feel quite fragile. Like a butterfly emerging from a chrysalis, you might need time to pause in the sun and dry out your wings, so that when the time comes you can fly.

I honestly think some people become fed up and frustrated and when in their eyes things are back to normal, and they would like you to bounce back and continue where you left off so to speak. But you and I know that is just not always the way it works.

I remember listening to one such person, deciding that they may be right, and once again hiding behind the façade of *I am fine*.

I then reverted to being that person who used to fly around the house trying to make it pristine for visitors. You remember what I said way back in the beginning about using negative distraction to back up the *I'm fine* statement, well, it was all too easy to fall straight back into that again. This ended in complete burnout, and we know what happens when I ignored glaringly obvious physical signs and paid no attention to the frightening thoughts in my head. It also had far-reaching consequences for those I lived with, as I had put self-care on the back burner, I ended up incapable of functioning properly. The frustration associated with this meant I was not a nice person for a while.

Sometimes it is difficult to ignore the very unhelpful voice in my head that takes great joy in reminding me that I am the carer, not the one to be cared for. But you and I now know that is just not true, and that the voices we should be listening to are the comforting ones of those who know us.

There is also a flip side to the input you may receive from those around you, and as I have found on my journey, there are some people who have some great advice.

As an expectant mum, I can remember almost drowning under the barrage of other mum's experiences and information that they were desperate to impart, and I can almost guarantee any other soon-to-be mum, in that position can relate to this.

I remember once, being sat on a bench, minding my own business, very obviously pregnant, when a lady came and sat next to me. When she saw my rather large bump, she started to tell me about how important it was to breathe and not to be a hero and take any and all drugs there were offered to me. It was like being attacked by a passing whirlwind. The manner, tone, and context of her advice were quite unhelpful.

In the same way, there will be people who will have been on a similar journey as you, who are caring for their child, and in the same way, they will want to give you advice. So how do you cope with that without getting overwhelmed?

The best direction I can give you for managing this is to share some words of wisdom from my own lovely Mum.

She once told me when people give you advice you don't have to take everything everybody says on board, just sieve it, pull out the bits that may be useful to you, and then just let the rest go.

I have always gone back to this piece of advice and it has always been helpful. You can even apply that in the early days when you are talking to family and friends, and they try and help by offering lots of suggestions and ideas.

Talking about friends and family and those who are your cheerleading squad, soak up the kind words they will have for you during this early period of recovery and beyond. Continue being honest with those around you, but even more importantly continue being honest with yourself. On those days, whether there is an obvious reason for the black cloud or not, reach out and share how you feel, whether that is chatting to someone in your support network, or having a good rant on a closed Facebook group. There is such a release to sharing it with someone. Sometimes when those difficult feelings and thoughts rise up it is difficult to see through the fog, and it is wonderful to listen to some wise words.

My birthday is coming up in about a month and although I know I can look forward to some pleasant distractions, I still feel a little nervous about the black cloud that hovers over me during that time. However, I have those around me who know me and are aware of how I am feeling, and don't have any expectations. They will remind me to practice what I preach when it comes to self-care. My son is one of the first who will remind me gently:

Mum, what do you say to me when I am struggling?

And it goes something like this:

I am so sorry you are feeling a bit icky, how about you go and put on your 'comfies' (self-explanatory – anything you may feel comfy in – joggers, fluffy onesies, the items of clothing that let it 'all hang out' and makes no apologies for it). I shall make you a cuppa, and we could watch one of your favourite shows, or play some card games. If you would just like me to be a comforting presence while you do your own thing, that would be fine. Whatever you fancy and may make you feel a little more human.

How will you respond when you have a day like this?

Perhaps there is someone you could call or something you could reach for from your comfort box. Maybe you can make time for a peaceful walk or a soak in the bath. You could have a look at some of the practical suggestions in Chapter 10 or make a list now of those things that will *gruntle* you.

I hope you will have some ideas of what you can do in those moments when you need to take some time out and take extra care of yourself and remember whatever you choose to do will be more beneficial if you allow yourself to do it guilt-free!

So Where Does That Leave Us?

We have looked at how we cope with those unhelpful comments and difficult days. I want to add that *bad days don't mean lost progress*. They really don't. Although during these times you may feel like you have taken a step backwards, these are still days during which you are healing.

They are still days that are further away from the trauma and closer to recovery. Hopefully, they are days where you can learn a little bit more about how you tick, how to look after yourself a little better, how to tune in to the useful voices, and most importantly, how to be at peace with who you are and where you are on your journey.

It will take time to get here and as I have said, in my experience, it is a process, but if you take nothing else away from this book – please let me reassure you that:

You are an extraordinary human being. You have been through hell and back looking after someone you love and seeing them suffer. At times you probably felt, utterly helpless. You deserve some kindness for yourself, after all the kindness you have showered on them.

...and remember:

Your body, your brain, your recovery in your own time!

After everything you have been through, and may still be going through, it should not be much of a surprise that you may have changed. You know what, this is completely normal and healthy, and accepting the fact is actually quite brave. We have learnt to look after ourselves and do that guilt-free, and now this is more of a priority than it was before, this can only bring about positive change.

In the next chapter I want to talk to you a little more about what that change may mean to you, and how you can learn to love this new person.

CHAPTER 17

The New You

IN THIS CHAPTER, I want to chat with you a little about change. As I have mentioned, the things we go through in life will change us. I am just about getting to the stage where I can entertain the idea that it is worthwhile being kind to this new person. I would like to show you how to do that too.

At some time or other, you may have gone for a brave new hairstyle. If you have, you might have experienced that moment when you catch a glimpse of someone in the mirror, and you do a double take because you did not recognise them for a second.

Don't you feel silly?

At the start of this new phase of recovery, it may be that you do not recognise yourself straight away, but I want to reassure you that I have found that that is natural and perfectly ok.

We have explored how it is so important to take care of ourselves while in the eye of the storm, but I think it is just as important to keep that up when we come out of the other side when perhaps it is not so obvious we need it. When we do this, we are more able to cope with setbacks and the new challenges we face as parents. There is a saying *"what does not kill you makes you stronger"*. Personally, I think a better one would be.

If you can survive being a parent, you are indestructible!

There was a time in the dim and distant past when I was very outgoing, and it did not take much to flick me into party mode.

The process of growing older, gaining more life experience, and living through the challenges that I faced changed me as a person and as a parent. I hope that these changes have mostly been positive ones and that I have grown in wisdom and understanding. I believe that is true for every parent who has supported their children through difficult times, and I am sure it is true for you too.

When it comes to facing challenges that have involved my children, I feel like I have not only changed but evolved. In more recent years, I definitely have not been the life and soul of the party. Indeed, that mode appears to have been switched off. I struggle a little with self-confidence, and I will certainly do anything to avoid confrontation. However, when it comes to those children of mine, it is almost like I became possessed for a while.

Say anything to me, upset me, hurt me, sadly I would probably turn around and apologise to you. But try anything with my offspring and you had better run for the hills, cos Mumma Bear is on the warpath.

It is in our human nature to second guess ourselves in just about everything, and when it comes to parenting it can sometimes feel like we are battered relentlessly with guilt that we are not doing enough or could have done things differently. It is a very strange thing and a contradiction in terms. but I believe that there is something excruciatingly painful yet strangely comforting about being amid trauma.

I discovered that during the stormy years, many people, even those I was close to, gave me a lot of leeway with regards to pretty much everything, including my behaviour. Although what we were going through was unimaginable to them, they knew it was bad, and that we were coping with a tsunami of issues. During this time, surprisingly little was expected of me. My family and friends were kind enough to recognise I had nothing left to give, and as such, I felt to some extent, I was off the hook.

I was in the eye of the storm, and during that time my focus was completely on my child and every waking hour was consumed by this. I am not sure whether at the time, I specifically gave myself permission to allow everything else to go to the dogs. I am sure that if I had done so, I may have been able to prevent some very unnecessary and misguided guilt.

I found that when things had calmed down and eventually dragged myself out of the woods, my sensitivity to just about everything had gone off the charts. I was tired and forgetful, to the extent of constantly losing everything.

I joke that I have spent hours upon hours looking for things in my life, but this was off the scale. Just how many times can you lose your keys and your phone in the time it takes to get ready to go out? On particularly bad days I would come back from a walk and find my keys in the outside of the door! I can almost feel you nod your head in that familiar way and saying, it's not just me then!

I was prone to tears at the slightest little thing, in fact, scratch that, the floodgates would open at the slightest little thing and I found myself a little scared at the outside world. The buffer I had when the trauma was raging was gone, and I was just on the cusp of starting on the long road to recovery. Suddenly my focus was no longer on one thing, but life had resumed, and suddenly I felt like I should participate in all the other things that daily living brings.

How do you do deal with the rude intrusions that worm their way into your head and trigger painful and difficult memories, and all without the familiar chemicals that in the past were helping you put one foot in front of another?

We talked briefly about the initial adrenalin rush that comes with dealing with traumatic situations, and that the same adrenalin carries you through and slightly takes the edge off reality. We need to be aware that at some point that adrenalin subsides, and for me, that is when I buckled.

I felt that people were thinking *her child is now in recovery so all is peachy and as such mum will also be feeling better*, and I started to beat myself up. That could not have been any further from the truth. I felt like a failure.

There is *GOOD NEWS!* After speaking with my family and friends since I have proof and can reassure you that the thoughts of those people close to me were quite the opposite.

To back that up further, I have had the privilege of hearing many parents' stories. They have also told me that when the person they were speaking with had picked their jaw off the floor, the recurring response was something along the lines of *I cannot imagine what you have been through! Are you getting any support?* Kindness, compassion, and a willingness to come alongside, even though they may not have understood your journey. For me hearing words such as these and having my feelings validated went a long way to aiding me in recovery.

Something else you may discover over here where the grass is just a little greener and more *GOOD NEWS* is that I believe a little bit of magic happens when we have been through trauma, and the best way I can describe my experience is this.

Imagine those video games where, when your character has got back up after a fight (notice I did not say win) they receive a reward and score enough points to buy some armour. The more times your character gets up the more armour he amasses. Therefore, each time he goes into the fight, he has a little more protection. On top of this, imagine this armour is forged in the magical mountains and is as light as air, so when your character goes back into the fight not only is he more protected, but he does not have to compensate for extra weight. Looking back, I was not aware of the armour I had collected. It must have been there, because life being life, we still have our battles, but we come out a lot healthier than we used to.

In fact, there have been times where we have faced situations that may have floored some. My husband and I have looked at each other and shrugged our shoulders in a *meh* kind of way. It is not to say we don't care; it just means we have dealt with worse and we have enough armour to go into the ring and knock it out of the park or at least be confident of surviving it.

I am not saying that it is easy or that there will not be days where you beat yourself up just a little bit, because as parents we always feel we could be doing more. We worry because we care so much.

There is a lovely quote from one of my favourite authors that I think sums this up perfectly.

'The fact that you worry about being a good parent means you are one already'- Jodi Picoult.

I received support and kind words from those around me with regards to my parenting, but I guess the trick is being kind enough to allow myself to believe them.

It is my experience that when you do, it can be incredibly healing, and makes it easier to be conscious of treating yourself well and accepting that you may have changed.

Remember, when you think about everything we have been and may still be going through, we can understand how this can take its toll. Even though we are stronger, when we come out at the other end, is it any surprise that we are altered, sometimes to an extent that we barely recognise ourselves. Everything you have been through or are going through will change you. And that is OK. By all means, carry on ferociously loving those close to you but try and leave some of that love for yourself. Carry on applying the self-care liberally, keep using those things in your well-being first aid kit, and be gentle with yourself.

Next time you catch a glimpse of yourself in the mirror and shrink back in shock at this person looking back at you, just remember:

Although that person looking back at you may have been to hell and back, they are still standing, they are utterly amazing, and they deserve a whole lot of love too.

You are a survivor

There was a day not so long ago that I recognised that survivor and felt that perhaps I could start to contemplate what may come next. In the next chapter, we will have more of a look at what change looked like for me practically, and how I dealt with making that big step back into the big bad world.

CHAPTER 18

Baby Steps

WHEN MY BOYS WERE more settled and things had calmed down, I decided to try and brave the big bad outside world and look for employment again. I learnt quite a bit during this time, mainly through trial and error. I discovered there was definitely a right and wrong way of approaching this. In order that you may avoid some of the pitfalls I came across, in this chapter I would like to share with you some of my experiences, and how when I found my feet, life outside the storm suddenly became full of possibilities once again.

When we finally turned a corner and the storm had passed, we suddenly had this deafening peace, and it was so unfamiliar and strangely unsettling. We used to have a poster on the wall in the kitchen when I was little. It was a picture of a kitten furiously trying to hang onto a branch with its little extended claws and underneath it said, *without trauma, my life would be empty.* I always thought it was very strange, but now I get it.

In previous chapters, we have talked a little about how to re-adjust to life, and how important it is to do this in your own time. We have explored the possibility that we may change, how to be happy with that change, and the importance of keeping up the habit of self-care. Then, as we enter a new stage of our life, we are more equipped to deal with new challenges.

When I got to this stage, my experience was that it was both exciting and terrifying in equal measures. I am no longer surprised that this is how I feel when I face anything new. Even now, it is how I felt about writing this book.

I had come to the realisation that I had changed, but at the time I was not sure how that was going to manifest itself.

In the past, I worked as a conference manager for the Forensic Science Society, and part of my job was organising huge conferences sometimes, with up to 500 CSI delegates. Looking back, the juggling I did was circus worthy. I had accommodation, speakers, seminars, gala dinners, and press conferences to organise, and the added pressure of ensuring everything fell within the strict guidelines of the Society. When I had been through the years looking after my children, I had no idea of whether that confident, savvy, organised woman still existed, because I not seen her for so long. I know that I had lost a lot of confidence, and that is still something I have to work on, but what about that person who could speak to anyone and was able to problem-solve like a pro?

This is what I found, and I hope it brings you a little comfort. She was still there, just slightly buried and somewhat rusty, but slowly I am unearthing her, and little by little that confidence is returning.

It would not surprise me if you have a similar experience when you get to the stage where you are ready to explore the world on the other side of the storm.

I had the opportunity to do something for myself, and that had not happened for a long time. The last eight years had been spent caring for my gorgeous boys and I had forgotten what it felt like to be a working woman with any responsibility.

A word of warning here. You remember what I said about not letting people dictate your recovery and doing things at your own pace, well this comes from a bitter lesson I learnt. If you are not ready, you stand the danger of early burnout. I went back to work before I was ready, and because I was still so fragile, when the slightest thing went wrong, I fell to pieces. This knocked my confidence and did me no good at all.

If I had gone back to work after years of a physical illness, I am sure allowances would have been made. The question is how you explain at an interview what you had been through, when that person sitting opposite you may have absolutely no experience of dealing with anything like it. They could not even possibly contemplate the effect it may have had on you.

As I did not yet have the confidence, I felt that if I shared anything personal with that person, they would see it as a sign of weakness. So, I said nothing. I did my legendary thing of once again becoming that actress with *I'm fine* as my default. What a blessing that both you and I now know better.

So, what happened when I was ready? When I listened to myself and decided it was time, a little bit of magic happened.

Suddenly I did not feel like my experience, and the fact I was still and would always be a little more delicate was a sign of weakness. I let myself believe that I was in fact incredibly strong and brave to be there right at that moment, having been through everything I had been through. That is exactly what you should believe about yourself.

There has been a thread that has been woven throughout these pages, and that is how incredibly beneficial it is, to be honest with those around you, and about how you felt along the journey. You do not have to tell people everything, just enough to set the scene. At my most recent interview, I did just that. Since my days as a conference manager, I realised I did not have that energy anymore to do that, so I trained as a Teaching Assistant working primarily with children with ASD and specialising in behavioural management. The job was working with a student with ASD in a mainstream setting. As the interview progressed, I knew that the question I had once dreaded would come up. *'Tell us more about the last eight years and why you have not worked.'*

And this is what I said, honest and simple and to the point. I explained I had spent the time looking after my two boys who had been extremely ill with severe mental health issues.

Their response nearly knocked me off my chair and went something like this.

'That is amazing, what an incredible mum you are. I cannot imagine what that must have been like. I would imagine you learnt so much that you could pass on to others.'

There you go, just another example that there is compassion even without understanding. Not only did I get the job, but they validated that experience of caring for my boys by asking my advice when helping other parents. I was able to help others who were navigating health issues with their children too.

I hope that this gives you a little comfort that what I have written here is not me just trying to boost your confidence, but that the outside world is very likely to validate how amazing you are as well.

When you get to this stage where you may be considering whether it was time to look at your options, whatever that means for you, it may be worth asking yourself some questions so that you may feel more prepared. To help these are some of the questions I asked myself.

What has changed for me?

Have I the energy I had previously?

Can I take anything else on while not letting anything slip, including time for myself?

What do I really want to do?

What have I learnt that I could use going forward?

I am sure you can think of plenty of questions of your own, but I think perhaps the most important thing to bear in mind is not to expect too much of yourself too quickly. It's all about baby steps, and do not forget to continue with the self-love and being gentle with yourself.

Even though through all of this I still felt delicate, having positive experiences really helped build my confidence and I hope you have many that will do that for you too!

With this newfound confidence, I was able to start looking into an idea I had many years before. We had been through so much as parents with little or no help, and I never wanted anyone in that situation to ever feel that helpless. As I explored how I might help I learnt a profound and life-changing lesson, and that is that there is incredible healing to be found in helping.

In the next chapter, I would love to share the story that led to just that.

CHAPTER 19

Healing in Helping

I CANNOT REMEMBER EXACTLY when it was that the thought first crossed my mind, but I think it may have been in one of those uneasy peaceful moments between battles when I had dared to think forward more than one day.

I remember saying to my husband that, when this is over, maybe there are others out there who are going through something similar, and who would appreciate someone to talk to. This stayed in the back of my mind for some time, and if I am honest, I did not think I could take anything on. I did not think I would be able to start, let alone sustain something worthwhile while I was still so delicate.

It was sometime later that a friend said to me. '*Do you think parents like you want to attend a support group run by Wonder Woman? I think they would much rather come and chat with someone who is as broken as they are.'*

Not long after that light bulb moment, that friend and I set out to organise and run a support group for parents who were looking after children with mental health issues.

During some research, I met with a wonderful lady called Wendy Minhinnett. She had set up her own group Rollercoaster Parent Support, which now supports over 700 members, and very kindly offered to act as our mentor.

We learnt lots of tips and tricks from talking to her and other professionals and charities. We also realised that being aware of the help in our locality meant we could potentially signpost our members to them for further help.

When we had everything in place, and with the backing and support of Rethink Mental Health, we opened the doors for our very first group.

I was extremely nervous and did not have any great expectations. When Wendy first set up, she had no one turn up for the first 3 months (and I have found that these things tend to work like that). However, the fact she had persevered and worked until she had been successful was and still is very encouraging and inspirational.

That first night 18 people walked through the door to attend our group. I had an agenda and had been told it was really important to lay down some rules concerning confidentiality, not speaking when others were, being respectful etc.

However, it quickly became apparent that the overwhelming need for these people who had joined together for the first time was just to be able to talk.

There is a lovely quote by C S Lewis and it goes like this: -

"Friendship is born at that moment when one person says to another: "What! You too?
I thought I was the only one!" - C S Lewis

For me, this is the cornerstone and the foundation that any peer support group should be built on and the single most important reason for having them.

Before I tell you a little more about the group, I would just want to take you back a moment to before the support group was up and running.

During this time, when we were researching what or who was available to offer support for the charity, we found ourselves at what was advertised as a parent carer meeting and it was not at all what I had expected. Picture if you will one of those rooms that you will find in any old church or community centre and then in the middle of that picture something that looked a little like a wonky round table with dozens of chairs around the outside.

I am not exactly sure what we had walked in on, but around this table, lots of frustrated people were trying to speak at once. They were understandably angry at their local council for closing down an art therapy group. Angry to the extent that they tried to enrol us into a group who were to demonstrate outside the council offices the following week.

It was chaired by a very charming and enthusiastic lady, but even she did not seem to be able to get a word in edgeways. As all this was happening another person was going around the table trying to get us to buy *raffle tickets*. Can you believe that? Pretty bizarre even by my standards, but it turned out that perhaps that meeting was one of the most important I ever attended.

I believe at certain times in our life God sends us pivotal moments. Moments that confirm we are moving in the right direction. They don't have to be accompanied by fireworks, sometimes it is just a gentle nudge. On this occasion, that moment just happened to be the conversation I had with the guy I had ended up sitting next to.

He looked as confused and dumbfounded as I felt and leant over and said, 'this is not really what I was expecting'! I came here for a bit of support.'

He had come to this meeting, hoping to find some respite in so much as being able to chat with like-minded people. He felt that yet again he had been let down and disappointed. In his experience receiving the support, he needed at the time might as well have been a universe away, if indeed it even existed. It was what I needed to hear. I realised I had to take that thought I had all those years ago and turn it into a reality, so the very next day I started working on the documents needed to set up a charity.

Before he left, and coincidentally at the same time as one of the ladies made a beeline for the old piano in the corner, I said I was in the process of setting up a support group and took some contact details from him. I promised I would drop him a line when we were up and running.

I then slunk out very shortly afterwards, sadly missing what I believed was going to be the after meeting singsong and leaving all the strange activity behind me.

I kept my promise, dropped him a line with all the group details, but was not sure whether he would respond or come to the group as he lived a considerable distance from where it was to be held.

He was among the first people to arrive along with his partner. When the time came to tell us a little of his background, and he will not mind me sharing this with you now, he described how earlier that week he had had to talk his child down from a bridge before getting back to the pub he owned for last orders. Incredibly this was part and parcel of normal life for him at the time.

I sat and listened as each of the parents shared their story and their fears and worries for their children's future. I was alarmed that every single one of them expressed a little guilt for being there! I realised there and then what these parents needed, as well as the chance to chat to others like themselves was the permission to be OK with not being OK. A reminder that they mattered as well as their child, and I know that you will recognise the importance of that now too.

The group as it stood then ran for a year and during that time, we learnt so much.

We learnt: -

- that sometimes a group with just two in can be just as beneficial;
- we all had ideas, tried, and tested methods that we could share and try;
- crying with someone is incredibly healing for both parties; and
- more often than not, we did not have any solutions to the issues parents were dealing with, but we were able to make the situation a little more tolerable just by being available to talk to.

Unfortunately, after about a year life got a little complicated on my side and I became ill. As we know it is the nature of these things that we are not always sure what caused the relapse. I practiced what I was preaching at the time, recognised I needed some time out for some rest, and with the full backing of my colleagues stepped back from the charity.

During this time life also offered new challenges for those I had previously been working with and I recognised and respected that they needed to follow alternative paths. Those trustees stepped down and although I keep in contact with our parents, the group as it was stopped meeting.

Finally, after a house move, that went anything but smoothly at the time, I once again found myself in the glorious situation of having some spare time on my hands.

Fast forward a couple of months and just one week before the lockdown measures were instigated, I had a meeting with Rethink Mental Health. I had decided to re-launch and rename the charity and this meeting was the first step in getting the funds I needed to do just that. As a support group at this time was not a viable option, I decided for the time being to restart the Facebook page and start working on new charity documents, and Parents in Mind was born.

Parents in Mind (PIM)

A phoenix from the flames if you will, and yes, we have had to go back to basics and be content with trying to support you virtually and yes, we are starting pretty much from scratch, but we are there right now if you need us. We will continue to work to support as many parents as we can and raise awareness that as carers, you are doing an incredibly difficult job and need support too.

I have shared all of this with you as it is as much part of this story as the trauma in previous years. Perhaps even more so as going on this journey has enabled me to heal in a way that countless trips to the therapist could never do.

Talking to amazing people about their stories, their battles, their tragedies, and triumphs have a strange way of putting the world into perspective as well as recognising the benefits of strength in numbers.

It is true that if you speak with enough people, you will always find someone who has been on a similar journey to you, and sometimes that gives us an opportunity to offer comfort through sharing. More importantly, talking to each other, crying, and laughing with each other, gives us something we all yearn for, and that is a true sense of purpose.

Our Facebook page *Parents in Mind* is up and running, and if you have a moment or need somewhere to go to rant or vent or just chat with like-minded parents, we would love to hear from you. We would also love to hear your stories, and any tips and tricks or good strategies that you have come across on the way that may help others.

On the subject of telling your story, I just wanted to include a brief chapter about just that. I want to show you why it can be so powerful not only for you but for others walking a similar path. Something I have found to be true time and time again is that you never know who you may meet on your journey, or who you could offer some comfort to.

CHAPTER 20

The Power of Your Story

I HAVE REALISED THAT we don't have to be perfect, we don't need to have it all together or be a superhero in order to reach out and help others.

I thought it would be nice to spend some time looking at that a little more in the hope it may give you a little more confidence when the time is right for you to take another step too.

I have a passion for, and I am drawn to, anything Japanese. I love the art, and the use of and passion for colour. I am intrigued by the crazy animation and the futuristic hi-tech side. I love the idea of starting the day with Rajio Taiso (warm-up exercises) in the fresh air, under cherry blossom trees, whatever your age. I love the food, especially sushi, but most of all it is the overriding attitude toward all living things that I find inspiring.

The Japanese refer to this aesthetic as Wabi-sabi. The definition is as follows:-

A world view centred on the acceptance of transience and imperfection. The aesthetic is sometimes described as one of beauty that is imperfect, impermanent, and incomplete.

There is a particular art form in Japan that goes on to encompass this ideal further called Kintsugi. There is a wonderful story behind this traditional craft, and it goes something like this.

It is believed this took place in the 15th Century when Ashikaga Yoshimasa was in power as the eighth Shogun.

One day he broke his favourite goblet and, not wanting to throw it away as it was precious to him, he sent it to be repaired. When it was returned to him it had been repaired with crude metal ligatures much like heavy staples.

Unsatisfied he then asked for some traditional craftsman to see if they could do a better job. Taking the broken pieces, they put them back together filling the cracks with lacquered resin and powdered gold thus making the cracks a beautiful addition to the original piece.

The Shogun was delighted to receive his goblet back, useable and bearing even more value.

In this story exists the wonderful idea that we should not throw away broken things because their brokenness can make them unique and precious.

The repair which highlights the beauty of the scars makes them even more valuable.

One of my outlets over the years has been my art. The medium I use is broken glass which I form into mosaic. The glass comes from craftsmen who create big pieces of stained glass such as windows. These pieces of glass that I use are offcuts and of no use to them and would be thrown away. I take these broken pieces and create something new from them. Quite simply it is making something broken beautiful. If you would like to see some of my creations, you could always pop over to my Facebook page @*Making Broken Beautiful* and say hello.

This not only refers to the medium and technique but more importantly to a story of hope and healing. Your scars, be they physical or psychological, are beautiful and you have every right to wear them with pride. They tell of real-life and survival. I believe it is quite simply the chaos and the brokenness that make us so qualified to reach out to others.

I am not saying that you need to go and shout your story from the rooftops, and it may be something that you don't want to or don't feel ready to share. That is absolutely fine. Only you know if and when you are ready to talk to others about your experiences, but as we have discussed sharing with others can be immensely helpful and healing for both parties.

The whole journey I have been on whilst writing this book has been amazing. I also hope that as a reader you have been on a journey with me too. True I have had to drag some of the chapters kicking and screaming into being and there have been days when the writing was hard and tedious. I have cried sometimes as I have re-visited scenarios and feelings. I have admonished myself more than just a few times and had strong words with myself about practicing what I preach. I have reconnected with parts of the past and made peace with some of the harder memories.

I spoke with Wendy yesterday, my friend and charity mentor who said, 'that must have been so healing, writing it all down, seeing where you are now in comparison to where you were.'

I think she hit the nail on the head.

Remember what we discussed about having those days where all you can do is write down one good thing that happened today? I think perhaps I shall do that every day from now on.

Recovery from trauma is strange, it is a little elusive and it creeps up on you, often without you realizing. It's only when we find ourselves saying things like, w*ell even a month ago, we would not have been able to do that* or *I don't remember the last time I had a whole week where I slept so well,* that we realise things are slowly getting better, and there are most definitely better days ahead.

You and I have been on an incredible journey together looking after our children, perhaps to the extent it was all we did, and after all the effort, we should not be surprised that we may still be a little wobbly.

I am sure you have seen those documentaries when you see a brand-new calf or foal being born. You then watch them as they try to stand up, then fall, then try again. On top of this, they are trying to co-ordinate all their limbs so that they are in the right place to enable them to stand firm. It takes a bit of time to literally find their feet and I still feel like that some days. But there are far more days when I wake up and stand strong, excited for what the day has in store and I hope you will find more days like that too.

We have looked at the fact that if you spend any time in a storm you are likely to come out of the other side a little windswept and weather worn. That is OK and it is also more than OK that you have changed.

My advice going forward would be to take each and every good day from now on as a win. Bank them for you and your children for a rainy day, knowing that a rainy day will be a little less dark and dreary than the last one.

You never know when you may get the opportunity to pass on this advice or you may have your own words of wisdom that could help another person, so in order that you are in the best possible place to do that, carry on applying that self-care.

Carry on doing what you can in the confidence that if it comes from a place of love you are doing all you can. Be kind to yourself and make sure you keep letting yourself be saturated by the kind, positive nurturing words I hope you have found in this book and from those around you.But more than anything please do yourself a huge favour and believe them, because you,

Dear Parent Carer, are an incredible human being and you deserve the same amount of love that you so selflessly give to your children.

About the Author

Ali Jeffries has a passion for working with parents who are caring for a child with mental health issues.

In 2012 her journey of navigating the system to get appropriate care for her children began, with many challenges and obstacles. Getting support for her children was extremely difficult but getting support for herself as their carer was nigh on impossible.

There was nothing set up to address this, so she decided that when things were calmer she would endeavour to ensure that in the future, parents who found themselves in a similar situation would have someone to talk to. Ali wants to offer peace of mind that they are not on their own.

In January 2019 she hosted her first parent support group so that parents could talk to like-minded people. They would have the opportunity to be signposted to professionals or charities that could support them further. In 2020 she re-launched as "Parents in Mind".

2020 sent our world into chaos with the onslaught of COVID 19 and as groups were no longer viable, she decided to get everything she had learnt down in writing, and this book, *Dear Parent Carer,* was born.

Ali has a background working with children with ASD, both in special schools and mainstream settings. Together with the knowledge, she has gained in her professional capacity and as a mum, she has put together a guide for parents by sharing tips and tricks and coaching them in the importance of self-care. She believes this is essential when you are caring for others.

Ali is also a stained-glass artist and believes this creative outlet has been a huge aid to recovery over the years. As well as displaying her work and receiving many commissions, she has held mosaic workshops to share those therapeutic benefits with others.

She lives in the East Midlands with her husband and youngest son and shares the house with an elderly Staffordshire bull terrier and her son's guinea pig, new lockdown kitten, and a somewhat crazy budgie.

You can contact Ali by going to the Facebook page @Parents in Mind or at www.alijeffries-author.co.uk.

Useful Contacts

Below are some contacts I have come across that may also help in your journey.

YoungMinds

Helpline: 0808 802 5544

www.youngminds.org.uk

Parents' Information Service gives advice to parents or carers who may be concerned about the mental health or emotional well-being of a child or young person. You can also find a guide to CAMHS.

Action for Children

www.actionforchildren.org.uk

parents.actionforchildren.org.uk

Down to Earth Parenting Advice you can trust and 1 to 1 chat.

Home-Start

www.home-start.org.uk

Home-Start volunteers help families with young children deal with the challenges they face.

Gingerbread

Single Parent Helpline: 0808 802 0925

www.gingerbread.org.uk

One Parent Families/Gingerbread is the leading national charity working to help lone parents and their children.

Netmums

www.netmums.com

A unique local network for mums or dads, offering a wealth of information on both a national and local level.

You can find additional information or any updates on any of the above by going to itv.com/thismorning/articles/parentinghelplines.

Charlie Waller Memorial Trust

www.charliewaller.org

Information on mental health for parents and carers.

Citizens Advice Bureau

www.citizensadvice.org

Free, confidential information and advice to assist people with money, legal, consumer, and other problems.

CAP (Christians against Poverty)

www.capuk.org

Christians against Poverty is a national organisation specialising in debt counselling for people in financial difficulty.

SENDIAS

www.kids.org.uk/sendiass

Services (formally known as Parent Partnership Services) offer information, advice, and support for parents/carers of children and young people with special educational needs and disabilities (SEND). There is a **SENDIAS** Service in every local authority.

CAMHS Child and Adolescent Mental Health Services

www.nhs.uk

NHS services that assesses and treats young people with emotional, behavioural, or mental health difficulties. You can enter your location to find details of services in your area.

National Autistic Society

www.autism.org.uk

This service provides impartial, confidential information and advice for autistic people, families, friends, and carers.

Calm

www.calm.com

Calm is an app that helps promote healthier sleep with guided meditations and sleep stories.

Devie

www.deviecoach.com

A free app that enables you to have mini chats to help you understand and manage your child's behaviour for toddlers and preschoolers.

Parents in Mind

Facebook Parents in Mind – PIM

A safe space to chat with other parents who are caring for a child with Mental Health issues and have the opportunity to be signposted to other services and charities that could help further.

Happiful Magazine

happiful.com

Happiful is a mental health and well-being magazine on a mission to create a healthier and happier society through inspiring life stories and positive news.

Mindfulness

This is an excellent introduction and a really useful book and CD.

Mindfulness. A Practical Guide to Finding Peace in a Frantic World by Danny Penman, J. Mark G. Williams, and Mark Williams.

Lightning Source UK Ltd.
Milton Keynes UK
UKHW020640010321
379583UK00013B/968